D1416644

# PRIESTHOOD
# IMPERILED

# PRIESTHOOD IMPERILED

## A CRITICAL EXAMINATION OF MINISTRY IN THE CATHOLIC CHURCH

BERNARD HÄRING, C.SS.R.

TRIUMPH™ BOOKS
Liguori, Missouri

Published by Triumph™ Books
Liguori, Missouri
An imprint of Liguori Publications

Scriptural citations are taken from the *New Revised Standard Version of the Bible,* copyright © 1989 by the Division of Christian Education of the National Council of the Churches of Christ in the USA. All rights reserved. Used with permission.

**Library of Congress Cataloging-in-Publication Data**

Häring, Bernhard, 1912– .
      [Heute Priester sein. English]
      Priesthood imperiled : a critical examination of ministry in the Catholic Church / Bernhard Häring. — 1st U.S. ed.
             p.   cm.
      Includes index.
      ISBN 0-89243-920-3
      1. Catholic Church—Clergy.   2. Priesthood.   3. Priesthood, Universal.
4. Pastoral theology—Catholic Church.  I. Title.
BX1912.H3713   1996
262'.142—dc20
                                      96-10631

Copyright © 1996 Bernard Häring
Printed in the United States of America
First U.S. Edition
96 97 98 99 00  5 4 3 2 1

# CONTENTS

The Nonviolent, Suffering, Liberating Servant of God •
Nonviolence and the Forgiveness of Sin •
The Priesthood of the Faithful and the Ministerial Priesthood

CHAPTER 11

## Behold the Handmaid of the Lord

Mary: Servant of God and Model for the Priesthood

# PREFACE

All of my priestly life I have reflected, taught, and written on the question: What kind of morality and moral theology are needed for the Church? My view of the moral quest was always influenced by, and understood within, the larger framework of another fundamental question: What kind of Church is needed in our present and future world? Inseparable from these two fundamental queries was a third question: What kind of minister is needed for our Church and world?

Because I have been happily and wholeheartedly a priest for fifty-six years and because, for most of that time, I have taught priests and seminarians, I was morally driven to address the kind of priest Jesus might have envisioned for the Church in her mission to embody and proclaim the saving power of God in our world.

In a very real and substantial way, I had to face and undergo major changes in priestly formation over the years at the same time that I was assisting others to do the same. In the process, it was imperative that I rethink the image of priesthood for our times. Thus, as I near the end of my life, it seems appropriate that I attempt in this little book to give witness to, and share my life experience with, my priestly peers and future priests, as well as with all Christians who minister to the Church and the world.

Even more, it is my fond hope that Christian adults engaged in the mission and ministries of the Church, and all those who care deeply about the priesthood, will read this book. I say this for two reasons. First, this book will deal with the special priestly calling mainly from the perspective of the basic vocation of all baptized Christians. Second, just as the priest cannot really understand his particular calling without a developing understanding of and a deepening reverence for the sublime and challenging vocation of all Christians, so, too, it is equally evident that a deeper, more integrated understanding of the meaning of ministry is essential for all committed Christians so that they may live out and evaluate their universal yet unique vocation in a more thoroughgoing way.

As moral theology wisely and necessarily reflects on all the major sources of theology, it is also expedient that we reflect upon Christian priesthood in a similar manner. Responses to this concern will, of necessity, be influenced by an understanding of anthropology, appropriate images of God and humanity for our times, and the nature and mission of the Church. While my theological reflections and ongoing search for truth include my experiences lived in various contexts over the years, they are nonetheless prompted by, and deeply grounded in, what I consider to be an indispensable starting point—namely, the vision of Jesus as we discover it in Scripture and in our lived tradition which has a long and complex history. These two sources of knowledge and wisdom serve as a catalyst for discerning what God requires of priestly people, and for how we shall together give shape to that requirement now and in the future.

It is not without a little fear and trepidation that I dare to share my hopes, endeavors, dreams, utopias, and personal commitment with you. Yet I do so all the same and with good reason, I believe. It seems to me that one man's dreams, should he indulge in them alone, remain merely dreams, but dreams shared by millions who have the capacity to realize them can largely determine the future of priestly life and ministry. In fact, my reflections, shared with people of many different languages and cultures, have been a vehicle in helping me refine my thoughts as well as clarify and assess my own commitments. In the process, I have come to believe more deeply that our Church and world are in dire need of hope and of courageous vision. In large part, the Church in the modern world also needs a healthy, informed, and healing public opinion.

When I entered the priesthood, the relationship between priest and laity could best be summed up in these queries: How do priests care for God's people, and how can they animate the faithful to cooperate with them? Today, however, the operative model is one of mutuality and collaboration, a model that asks an entirely different question: How do priests cooperate with both their bishops and the laity? This is the operative lens through which I have envisioned a different priesthood. It is the lens through which I see all of us searching together in a mutual quest to better know and understand God's salvific power and grace for the Church and the world.

The author wishes to thank Joyce Gadoua, CSJ, for her assistance in the preparation of the English translation of this book.

BERNARD HÄRING

# INTRODUCTION

Recently, I came across an article with the shocking headline: JESUS DID NOT WANT PRIESTS. As an elderly priest who has tried all his life to help people develop a spirit of peace, joy, and inner strength, I must say that I was initially irritated by this headline. However, as I proceeded to read the article, I discovered that the Catholic theologian who authored it had no intention of voicing opposition to the priesthood. Rather, with good arguments, he challenged readers to ponder a more insightful question, namely, "What did Christ really intend when he chose and sent apostles and disciples to preach the Good News to everyone?"

Subsequently, that article prompted me to ask several active Catholics whether or not Jesus truly wanted the priesthood. They answered my question by posing one of their own: "What image of priesthood do you think corresponds to the intention of Jesus?" While their question at least implicitly revealed a belief that Jesus had a vision for the priesthood, what shape that priesthood should take was tossed back to me to explain.

Not to be thwarted in my quest to engage these adults in reflection, I reworked my original question in a more concrete way and volleyed back with, "Whom might you identify as the priestly ideal Jesus might have envisioned?" The first responder said, "I would think of men like Bishop Jacques Gaillot, who is an honest, straightforward apostle of peace and thoroughly dedicated to people on the margins of life."

Following a recent lecture I gave to a gathering of several hundred peace activists, I unequivocally stated that a Christian, and especially a priest who does not radiate peace and who does not promote peace, nonviolence, and an all-embracing justice, is worth nothing. From the audience came an immediate challenge with a familiar ring: "What about the removal of Bishop Gaillot, who, in France, was the only bishop who took a clear position against nuclear arms while ever remaining on the side of the outcast and the despised?" More tentatively, I said, "It seems that a Christian, thoroughly dedicated to evangelical nonviolence, will of necessity be put at risk." It is a risk, I believe, that finds its parallel in the prophets of old, but most especially in Jesus, the Prophet and Model for all times.

And so, dear reader, I invite you also to share in this quest for deeper understanding of what Jesus meant when he called believers to embody his paschal life and proclaim the final victory of peace in and through the Resurrection. In so doing, we shall look to Scripture and, equally important, to history, since Jesus, who was, who came, and who will come, teaches us in view of the whole of salvation history.

In fact, a major reason for probing Scripture (apart from the important task of recovering its original meaning in its different historical contexts) is to discover via a new hermeneutics (the science of interpreting the Scriptures) what the Good News means today, and how these understandings might impact the meaning of priestly ministry now and in the future. Hence, this new hermeneutics requires we understand and appropriate the signs of the times as an integral part of this conversation if we are to properly discern the kind of priesthood Jesus might have imagined.

This is particularly important, since under the heading of "priest," we find virtually nothing of relevance in the Christian Scriptures precisely because the term did not yet exist at the time in which the Scriptures were written and compiled. Ultimately, what matters is not the specific word itself but rather the phenomenon of the priesthood as an historical outcome in a specifically Christian sense that originates in, and is attributed to, the life and ministry of Jesus himself.

## CHAPTER 1

# PERSONAL EXPERIENCES ON THE ROAD

Consciously or otherwise, our life experiences influence our thinking and our perceptions of reality. Reflection on both positive and negative experiences can be a fruitful exercise in understanding more deeply how God has been present and actively guiding us on our journey of faith. To that end, as I complete fifty-six years of priestly life, I reflect here upon my own experiences, and how they have helped me to discover and continue to develop my priestly calling.

### Discovering My Vocation

From the outset, one thing is sure: My childhood experiences with the local pastor, an average man by all standards, elicited neither the idea nor the desire to model myself after him. However, in those days, by virtue of ordination, the pastor was perceived by the flock as a superior being, a kind of lord, and as one of the most esteemed persons in the town, one who had the final word on everything, be it right or wrong.

Early in my childhood I had a very frightening experience with the pastor's dog, who, for whatever reason, took a strong dislike to me. Unlike the children whom the pastor disciplined so severely in class, his vicious dog was allowed to roam freely. Unfortunately, I had to pass the rectory on my way to school, and in times when I was alone, I armed myself with stones to defend myself against any potential assault.

One such day, the pastor's dog made a show of his "superiority" and attacked me, lacerating my private parts. In terror, I ran home to my mother, crying in pain the whole way. After tending to my wounds, my mother immediately took me back to the rectory and asked to see the pastor so that he could witness firsthand what his ferocious dog had done to me. His inhospitable housekeeper icily replied, "Asor knows his enemies!" Imagine!

However, I am happy to say that when the pastor saw me in such distress, he became quite sensitive, tried to console me, and gave my mother the means to buy a new pair of trousers. Years later when I preached a retreat for priests, I developed a whole meditation on "The Pastor's Dog" based on that initial encounter.

Unfortunately, that experience was not to be my last with this dog. In a period of starvation in postwar Germany, I was a young, war-weary priest who had returned to the area to provide Lenten services. When I saw that same malicious dog, fattened by age and overindulgence, I became inwardly angry. Even though I did not give any exterior sign of my aversion, the dog was nevertheless poised again to attack, and did so, as I returned from the confessional around midnight. In total darkness, I was waiting at the door of the rectory nearest the garden where the dog roamed and barked fiercely, hoping that someone would hear him. Since no one took notice, I opened the door and immediately the huge dog was at my throat. In shock, I cried out, but again to my surprise and disbelief, I was told upon entering, "The dog never harms anyone." Having been to many rectories since that time, I must say I have come across many friendly dogs who were mirror images of friendly pastors just as Asor mirrored his master.

My first real experience with the local pastor as teacher occurred when I participated in his religious education classes. A very strict disciplinarian, he was a furious and impatient man who used corporal punishment as a way of controlling and managing his students, not unlike many schoolmasters of his day. For this reason, among others, I was neither drawn to him as a person nor impressed by his manner of teaching the Catholic faith.

At the age of nine, I and my classmates were being prepared for our first confession, which turned out to be a very unhappy experience for me. To ensure that we would make a complete confession, the pastor told us this dreadful story that scared me out of my wits:

> An old monk died under the guise of holiness. After the "Requiem," the Abbot began the celebration of praise, but then a loud cry came from the coffin: "Stop this nonsense! I am in hell." "Why is this so?" the Abbot asked. The old man replied, "At my first confession, out of shame, I omitted a sin."

So frightened was I that I wrote a litany of real and imaginary sins and began confessing them with a childlike hope of appeasing a punishing God who, I thought, might otherwise send me to hell. Even though the pastor stopped me, whatever enthusiasm I may have had for the sacrament vanished quickly. That terrible experience had the effect of making me excessively scrupulous with all the unhealthy side effects such an attitude can bring, until a wise and wholesome confessor from a nearby convent rescued me.

In contrast to that experience, I have fond memories of my very wise mother who, on each long winter evening, read uplifting passages from the New Testament, stories of the lives of saints, and especially stories about missionaries that were appropriate to my age and development. In fact, my parents were deeply interested in the reports about the foreign missions. Their love and concern for missionary life was the seed that nurtured a youthful desire in me to become a missionary and preach the Good News in Africa or Asia, an aspiration that was a happy blend of youthful romanticism and of a genuine understanding of what it meant to preach the Gospel.

When I was ten, the pastor did somewhat better in preparing me for my First Communion. Next to my mother, it was my sister Constantine who truly helped me the most. My mother had entrusted me to Constantine to lovingly prepare me, such that on the day of my First Communion I felt inwardly confident to tell her, "I want to become a saint." No small ambition for sure, but my sister, having the heart and wisdom of a true and encouraging catechist, simply said, "Why not?" In my view, she was light-years ahead of the pastor in proclaiming the good news of my salvation already in progress. Without a doubt, she was well on the road of Christ, and at the age of fifty-one she died in holy joy as a Franciscan sister.

Nearing twelve, I approached my mother in a moment of solitude and asked, "What would you say if I became a missionary even though I know I am far from what a model should be?" With a look of sheer love and kindness, she fanned my zeal by saying, "Bernard, no saint has ever fallen from heaven. What was possible for others will also be possible for you with God's help." From that point on, I firmly held to my dream of becoming a missionary. At this time, however, the concept of "priest" eluded me. The visible reality of the local pastor certainly did not attract me, but the idea of a missionary preaching the Gospel filled my youthful mind with wonderful fantasies. Behind that hope remained my original query, "Why not try to become a saint?"

Shortly thereafter, my missionary hopes were greatly strengthened by the Redemptorists who came to preach a mission at my parish. I was especially impressed with Father Leonard Eckl, who later became a missionary himself and was elected Provincial Superior of the Redemptorists in Brazil. He had a special charism for awakening and furthering religious vocations in the young. His stories about traveling missionaries on horseback celebrating the sacraments and preaching a God of love in several parts of that country greatly enlivened my interest and strengthened my youthful resolve.

Years later, as I neared completion of my baccalaureate, I had given some thought to becoming a Jesuit missionary out of reverence for their great missionary zeal to be all things to all people in Asian lands. When I inquired about their formation program, I was told that, following the novitiate, two different tracks were offered. Gifted students were encouraged to become professors, while average students were invited to become missionaries. Knowing this, my interest in the Jesuits vanished, because I wanted, but did not get, the assurance that I would become a missionary and not a professor.

Abandoning that pursuit, I then sought the advice of the Provincial Superior of the Redemptorists and asked if he could guarantee I would have a missionary's life. Quite seriously, he said that he could offer me a ninety percent chance of realizing my dream. Convinced, I entered and completed my novitiate and shortly thereafter was instructed to learn Portuguese and study Brazilian culture. By the time I was ordained, I was well-groomed for missionary life and was happily convinced that this would be the particular way in which I would live out my priesthood.

## My First Mass

Together with my friend and cousin John Flad, I was ordained in May of 1939. In fact, when I began theological studies, John's mother (who was my godmother) said to him, "If your friend Bernard dares to study, why not you?" I might add that I was always perceived as being more daring than he, and furthermore, I was not considered to be a very good boy at that. What is interesting is that, well before the changes brought about by Vatican II, John and

I were already fervent advocates of liturgical renewal. Therefore, having gone through the seminary together, it was unbelievable to us that we could not concelebrate our first Mass together. We were not, however, rebellious, but we were mildly critical about the arrangements. Unfortunately, we each celebrated our own Mass, one after the other, in our home parish.

It rained heavily throughout that day, so we asked ourselves what this could mean. Since John and I were optimistic by nature, we decided that the rain was a symbol of God's grace showering us with what we needed for a fruitful life.

Shortly thereafter, when it was time for me to purchase a boat ticket for Brazil, my Provincial Superior knocked at my door, surprising me and causing me to wonder why I was receiving this particular honor. This man was the selfsame Superior who, six years earlier, had told me I need not fear becoming a professor and who, after first vows, directed me to study Portuguese and Brazilian culture. I came to see that the gracious rain of my ordination was more like cold water on my head as I heard my Superior's sobering words: "When your professors heard that you were appointed for Brazil, they became very angry with me. They want you to study for a doctorate in moral theology." Taken aback, I replied that such a request would have been my very last choice. Moreover, I made it quite clear that I disliked nothing more than studying in depth the kind of moral theology I had been taught. My superior immediately responded, "Therefore, we want this to change. Moreover, you are not meant to go to Rome to study. You can choose between Tübingen and Munich."

While I appreciated my professors' enormous trust in my intellectual capabilities, I was still very disappointed that my own plans and dreams had dissolved in that moment. Only much later did I realize what an enormous missionary task my Superior presented to me—to do my best so that moral teaching would truly be an integral part of proclaiming the Good News of God's saving power and presence to all. Moreover, little did I know at the time that my studies and war experiences would later afford me many global opportunities to truly be the missionary I dreamed of being.

## In the Medical Service

Given the choice of universities, I decided to study in Munich under Professor Theodore Steinbuckel, who was himself a pioneer in the renewal of moral theology. As a theme for my doctoral dissertation, I was given "The Sacred and the Good: The Relationship between Religion and Morals." However, just as I was about to embark upon this quest, I was one of the first priests to be drafted into the German army. As stipulated in the Concordat, priests could be called up to serve but only as medical personnel. The training unit to which I was assigned was composed almost entirely of priests, doctors, and medical students. Among us, there was a spirit of friendship that was as strong as our deep aversion to the war.

One rather simpleminded lance corporal in my unit had a tremendous superiority complex. On one occasion, he made a major show of it by commanding a priest to run to the other end of the field and cry out, "I am an idiot." The priest obeyed his command, and with consummate pleasure, yelled for all to hear, "Indeed, Corporal, you are right. You are an idiot!" His risky reply gave us all a much-needed laugh, and it also served to deepen the camaraderie among us. Moreover, it had the effect of making the hard-liners realize that priests were neither stupid nor cowards. Nor were they humorless.

As trained medics, we had it drilled into us never to minister in any priestly way, under any circumstance. Violation of this order could have yielded a maximum punishment of nine years in prison. I decided that I would ignore this order every time an opportunity presented itself for me to exercise my priestly calling, thus rekindling my earlier reputation as a "bad boy." In the protracted war on the Russian front, I served in the infantry as a medical sergeant. On many occasions, I brought back wounded men from the front and, at all times, was available to anyone who needed medi-

cal assistance. My being totally available enabled the men to see that
I was truly "one of them," and it was also a way of building trust
among them.

On the other hand, there were also a number of fanatic party-
men who never failed to show their contempt for priests. One day,
a captain insulted me in the presence of many soldiers. I sternly
replied, "If one day you should cry for help, I shall be there. Don't
forget it!" Some weeks later, as it turned out, I brought this very
captain back from the front, risking my life for him, and I bound
up his wounds as best I could. With tears in his eyes, he asked
forgiveness for insulting me, and from that singular confessional
experience, the term "one of us" took on even deeper meaning for
me, a meaning that would deepen throughout the war.

As Christ, the Son of Man was "one of us" in a universal way,
I, too, with deep conviction, chose to cross all confessional and
national lines. During the winter of 1940–41, my company was in
Normandy, where, at the outset, many French families and local
priests invited me into the circle of their friendship. Against the
laws of the Nazi regime, I chose to celebrate a solemn Mass in the
Cathedral of Bayeux every Sunday for our regiment and for the
French civilian population in that area. Given the spiritual hun-
gers in wartime, participation increased weekly. Had they any idea
of the risk I was taking in exercising my ministry?

One Sunday I bicycled into town and was met by the local
commander of Bayeux, who called me to him. Warily, I approached
him, wondering if he would proceed against this transgressor of
the law. To my joy and relief, he greeted me warmly and said he,
too, would assist in the celebration. Moreover, he asked me if I
would like him to send the regiment's music corps to add greater
solemnity to participation in the Mass. Having agreed, he then issued an order that I was to be brought to the Cathedral by car in
the future. Knowing how unjust this law was, the commander
showed a spirit of righteousness and courage in overriding it for
the good of all.

In the ensuing months, denominational lines broke down rather quickly. One day, a group of Protestant soldiers approached me and asked if I would organize an evening Bible study with them. For as long as I was with that unit, we met regularly and our friendship deepened. On the eve of the outset of the Russian war, I took it upon myself to celebrate the Eucharist and grant general absolution to soldiers of all faiths, most of whom participated. Given the seriousness of the situation, and because all of us were one in Christ Jesus, I found it unthinkable, in fact, totally abhorrent, to uphold and maintain any distinctions between Catholics and Protestants. Consequently, all the men, regardless of their faith persuasions, felt called to share in communion. At another time, I told my Protestant friends that their official pastor would be coming for a service, but their reply was, "There really is no reason to make any changes for us because you are 'one of us.'" Being one among others was a great joy and privilege unlike anything else for me in wartime, and this experience was to be repeated time and again.

I had wonderful opportunities for providing medical and spiritual assistance to many Russian Orthodox and Ukrainian people as well. Together, we celebrated a very moving experience of the rite of baptism for a great number of young and older children. Shortly thereafter, when I told a few women that I would come to celebrate the Eucharist on Sunday of that week, the news spread like wildfire, and scores of people, longing for the joy of the sacrament, came and participated.

Near the end of that diabolic war, I was a prisoner of war in a camp located in Poland. Members of a local Polish parish, whose sick I had earlier cared for and whose children I had baptized, decided they would rescue me and make me their pastor. Again I experienced the profound meaning of "one of us," an event in which I truly saw, through the eyes of faith, the light of Christ who understood Himself as "Son of Man," as "one of us."

### *"Is It Possible that God Sends a Priest to Me?"*

On one of the cruelest days on the Russian front, I became totally exhausted from retrieving scores of wounded and dying men. Hoping to rest and recover, I began digging a foxhole in clear sight of the "enemy." No sooner had I begun than I heard a cry from a distance: "*Sanitater* [medic], help me!" Humanly and militarily speaking, I could have excused myself. First, I felt I had totally expended my energies; and second, the man crying out was not of my unit, not "one of us." Suddenly, however, I understood quite well that he was "one of us," one who, like all of us, needed me as a priest. Mustering some hidden reserve of energy, I searched for the man for ten minutes in an open field under the gaze of Russian soldiers. To this day, I still wonder why they did not kill me. Perhaps they realized I was a medic, and respecting international law, let me pass. For me, it was never a case of caring less for the enemy on the battlefront. The priest knows no boundaries, and by their professional ethos, medics are men for others without distinction.

When I reached the wounded man, I attempted to help him but soon realized I could do nothing to save his life. With regret I said, "As a medic, I am too late, but as a priest, I am here in the nick of time." Wide-eyed with surprise, the soldier asked, "Is it possible that God sends a priest to me, a sinner?" He was even more astounded when I told him I had brought the Body of Christ for his last journey. Later, I informed his family about his death, and a priest who was a cousin of the man said, "What a miracle! My cousin had left the Church because of a great injustice committed against him by his parish priest, and he never found his way back. His mother has been praying day and night for his return."

Priests who are not persons for others are living contradictions of their calling. It is only when they respond to human need as it is presented to them, in whatever circumstances they find themselves, that they discover their true identity in Christ, the Son of Man, who was at all times "one of us."

Personally, it was also gratifying to hear Russians, Ukrainians, and Poles say, "Father Häring is 'one of us.'" While it was not an extraordinary remark by any means, it was, however, an important confirmation of my identity, and a challenge for me to continue to deepen and develop my priestly identity throughout my life.

## Among the Refugees

Shortly after the war, my missionary hopes were actualized among the victims of war. I and some of my priestly peers spent a few years preaching the Gospel to homeless Catholic refugees in Germany who lived in areas that, up to that time, were exclusively Protestant. No Catholic church or parish organization of any kind existed in those days. For each of the years I was there, I spent approximately ten weeks visiting the same areas with three other priests, but each of us also took individual responsibility for particular towns and villages.

Initially, we visited each family in a given area, and sometimes the Protestant pastor would offer his church in which to gather for celebration. More often than not, however, we rented a dance hall or a large room to accommodate our needs. Our living arrangements (where we would eat and what floor we would sleep on) were largely determined by the refugees themselves.

In one little town, none of the Catholic refugees invited me to sleep in their home, so I went to a Protestant innkeeper who offered me lodging normally inhabited by beggars and vagabonds. Not surprisingly, I saw that the bed linens had not been changed for a very long time. Since beggars could not pay, the innkeeper did not bother to make the place hospitable. When the family of a Protestant schoolteacher found out I was staying there, they changed the linen, invited me to dinner, and even notified Catholic refugees about my lodging conditions. Thanks to that event, there was enormous participation on the part of the refugees who were most eager to assist me.

Before I undertook this particular ministry, with priestly fervor I had prepared sixteen sermons on major Christian themes, but I never used any of them. Having lived so closely with the poor, I soon came to realize that the best way to proclaim the Word was to first listen to *their* worries, hopes, and joys.

It was in those lean and trying years that I began to write my thoughts, which culminated in the three-volume work *The Law of Christ*. Without those war and postwar experiences of sharing life with the needful and the poor, the text would have been very different.

Truly, it was in those times that I came to more deeply understand the person and ministry of Jesus, who traveled through Galilean towns and villages preaching the Good News to the poor while never knowing where he would lay his head. Aiding and evangelizing soldiers and refugees became a root experience for me. The eighteen African countries where I served intermittently some twenty years after the Second Vatican Council shaped my outlook, ideas, and approaches to ministry in the Third World, and realized my earlier missionary hopes a hundredfold.

These life-changing and deeply challenging experiences alerted me to fundamental problems I would never have truly understood had I not lived among the poor. They also deepened my understanding of the role of the priest as disciple of Christ. For in fact, how can we truly share the Gospel message with people in dire need if we are not willing to partake of their style and poverty of life? Knowing about poverty and living it are two different things. Becoming a disciple of the Son of Man requires that we meditate daily in the here and now, in our lived context, on what it means to be called "one of us." All this has very much to do with how we understand what "knowing Christ" means. It is only in helping the poor, the outcast, the deprived, as well as the more fortunate, that we truly come to "know" Christ Jesus.

## Awakening Vocations

Finding ways to awaken and nurture missionary vocations among the refugees was one of our most necessary and useful ministerial objectives. Realizing those objectives reminded me of Saint Paul and his missionary cohorts, who never left a place until they had found and instructed people who were capable of creating and developing communities of believers and who would continue their work. In each place, we were able to identify men and women who were willing to accompany us, and when necessary, introduce us to families.

My first experience in identifying potential lay persons for this ministry was in a Protestant and sometimes hostile area where displaced refugees lived. There I was fortunate to have two older saintly women and a twenty-two-year-old woman named Matje. While the two older women were most dedicated, I found that they needed to unlearn a few things. In a persistent manner, they urged me not to visit a particular Catholic family whom they considered unexemplary in many ways. Each time they brought it up, I explained to them, with utmost patience and kindness, that the central focus of Jesus' mission was to search for these particular kinds of people. By the end of the week, both of these women were astonished by what had happened. They said, "All those whom we considered hopeless have participated fully and have become new people."

Matje, who was a most unusual young woman, was the only member of her family who cared about the Catholic faith. In total openness to the saving Christ, she listened to the Word and made it her own. Shortly afterward, having made a promise to God, she revealed it to me: "If I can win my family back to the Church, I will become a missionary." As it turned out, she succeeded marvelously on both counts. Not only did she bring back her mother and sister in my first stay in that area, but she had also brought back her father and brother when I returned on my third trip. Soon thereafter, she became a Benedictine missionary and ministered in a marvelous way to the people of Tanzania. Many years later when we both had cancer, we met again in Germany. In spite of her illness (to which she succumbed shortly after visiting me), her radiance and joy never diminished. She was indeed a truly wonderful apostle.

In the next town, a refugee and a teacher from Silesia, who was my best helper, also addressed "hopeless cases" for which he thought all efforts would be wasted. It was extremely difficult for him to accept my oft-repeated remarks about Jesus who never entertained a discriminatory attitude toward anyone. When visitation was at an end, my helper told me of a Catholic woman and mother of six children who had become infamous in the town. She was engaged in prostitution with American soldiers. My helper exclaimed, "As a man of honor, surely you will not enter her house!" Not to be deterred in my quest to carry out Jesus' mission, I replied, "Since we are both men of honor, we can try to visit her together." Upon entering, we found her in the company of another woman who was also involved in prostitution. Seemingly angered by our presence, she spewed out a series of expletives that, up to that time, I had never heard. My friend said to me, "Did I not tell you so?" "Perhaps," I said, "we deserved her scorn, since had we not harbored contempt for her in our own hearts?" That evening, much to her surprise, I visited her again when she was alone with her children, and I was friendly with her as if nothing had happened. After a brief chat, she promised to come twice to our celebrations since I had come twice to visit with her. She surpassed her original offering and walked five miles with her older children to attend every evening.

A year later when I returned, the old teacher who had become my friend and generous helper said, "You were right. She has become a new person, and her children have also changed for the better." This was good news in abundance because, first of all, this poor single parent was deeply humiliated by her verbal abuse, which (contrary to what we originally thought) was motivated not by antagonism toward us, but rather by extreme deprivation. Second, good people were found to assist her out of her misery and into a new and better life. Last but not least, my helper underwent a conversion of heart, having understood from this experience that, like Jesus, ministering first and foremost to those considered to be outcasts, those on the fringes of society, was central to his calling.

Indeed, missionary activity is a "contaminating" endeavor in that we must get our hands and feet soiled in the mud of human misery if we are to participate in the benevolent and saving power of Christ. Ministering among the most needful is also a very important avenue for discovering, awakening, and nurturing missionary vocations among the poor as well as among others of more abundant means.

Compared to the apostolic activities of the early Church, on the plus side, we tried to build charismatic communities of faith everywhere we went. Whereas the first Christians never left a small community until it was provided with a Eucharistic minister, we, in contrast, and because of a peculiar tradition and strictures of canon law, left every community priestless. Yet even without the Eucharist, at the very least, missionary zeal developed in those impoverished areas. While God had also blessed me with the capacity to foster religious and priestly vocations during that time, that is not the point I wish to stress. More important is the priestly task of raising consciousness among lay people to their baptismal call to minister in the Church and society. Of equal importance is the responsibility of collaborating with the faithful to discern the needs of the times, to discover what ministries they are best suited for, given their particular gifts and talents, and, finally, to support them in their chosen ministries.

### Side by Side with the Sick

Needing a second surgery for throat cancer in 1977, I decided to go to one of the poorest hospitals in Colleferro (south of Rome), where the surgeon who discovered my cancer practiced his profession. He had learned an innovative procedure in the United States, which could only be performed on nonsmokers. As his first candidate, I saw this as a tremendous opportunity not only for myself but also for the doctor to test the merits of this technique. While my personal motivation in this respect may not have been entirely altruistic, I was thrilled to have the privilege of being among the poor, as "one of us."

Technically speaking, the hospital was first rate, but by contrast, there were many very poor and seriously ill people with few means. A group of charismatics came daily to provide newcomers with whatever they needed. They offered me the simplest gift of cutlery because they realized I had no idea I was supposed to provide my own. As they did for all poor people, they brought me a bouquet of flowers to brighten my room and my spirits. Even the sick welcomed me. One old woman in the next room came every day and sang a beautiful song. In a humorous vein, she remarked, "I am deaf and you are mute. We are all the same." Upon reflection, I have come to see that the gifts of the poor, expressed in a spirit of affability and true friendship, are more profound and more important than extraordinary comforts.

Completely mute, I learned to communicate quite well through body language and writing. When the most difficult period of my convalescence was over, much to my surprise, lay nursing staff and patients alike came to me to celebrate the sacrament of reconciliation. From this experience, I realized the more that, even in illness, barriers can be overcome, and one can still bring comfort to others.

The experience of living without a larynx these past fifteen years has been, in one sense, a real gift, because it has afforded me many wonderful opportunities I might otherwise not have had to comfort the sick, especially those who suffer in a similar way. I say this because when a perfectly healthy person tries to comfort and encourage the sick, it is possible that the ailing might react with:

"It's easy for you to talk. How can you really understand my situation?" I believe that a priest who has never suffered illness or has not had a physical loss similar to his patients' cannot as readily understand or deeply express genuine compassion as a priest who has.

Over the years, I have come to dwell more and more upon the words of the prophet Isaiah: "I have heard your prayer, I have seen your tears; indeed, I will heal you" (2 Kings 20:5). I find deeper meaning in these words precisely because my own illness became the vehicle that united me to the suffering of others; I could truly understand and share in their prayer, their tears, and their hope for healing. Also the second chapter of Hebrews relates Christ's sufferings intimately with his kinship to us all. That is, God has made Christ, our brother, perfect through suffering. I believe I have been privileged to "know" this Christ, my brother, fellow sufferer, and healer of all, and I have also come to understand the meaning of his ministry in ways I might never have understood had I not suffered deeply myself.

In the school of suffering, Jesus, as kin to us all, learned not only obedience to what God required, but also compassion in a special way (Hebrews 5:8-9). Not only by his words but also by his example, Jesus teaches us: "Be merciful, just as your Father is merciful" (Luke 6:36). The deepest meaning of Christ's sacrifice unto death is understood as bearing the burden of the sins of humanity (Hebrews 9:28), by sharing in people's suffering with infinite compassion. By his passion, Christ has become the supreme sacrament, the foremost communicator of the Father's compassion. Therefore, it is not only appropriate but necessary that the priest should also suffer, and by suffering, learn evermore to become more truly compassionate to all, most especially to the sick.

### *"Heal the Sick!"*

Throughout the centuries, the Church has taught and promoted pastoral and medical care for the sick. All around the globe, she has built hospitals for the cure and healing of the sick. Loving care of the sick has been her preeminent testimony of merciful love. It was the holy and inspired priest Saint Vincent de Paul, who, in rising above the cultural taboos of his day, released the energies and talents of thousands of vowed religious women to minister to the sick. Loving care and presence of holy women and men is, in itself, a healing factor.

However, in the past few centuries, an unhealthy polarization developed in which proclaiming the Good News became separated from the ministry of healing. There seemed to have been two institutions of the Church operating side by side, one for evangelization and one for healing. Even more serious was the prevalence of a dangerous and wounding moralism divorced from biblical faith that developed especially in the post-Tridentine era. This unhealthy turn of events spawned a series of severe noogenic and psychogenic neuroses, sometimes referred to as ecclesiogenic neurosis and psychosis. By contrast, it must be emphatically stated that a genuine faith and moral teaching rooted in New Testament faith was never, in any case, the cause of such mental illness. Rather, true faith rightly lived, proclaimed, and witnessed to, always embodies a unique healing power.

A careful development of the therapeutic dimension of faith and Christian morality has been, and continues to be, a major concern of mine. The totality of faith cannot be reduced to mere adherence to a body of truths (beliefs) taught by the Church. Basically, faith in its truest and most profound sense is a saving and healing *relationship* with God. Thus, care for healthy and healing relationships and the development of wholesome structures of life are central to a living faith. It is essential that priests, and all those who minister to others in the service of the Gospel, be well instructed and interiorly formed by these insights.

Some forty years ago when I was in Rome, a young woman, in the process of completing her final exams at the university, became ugly, violent, and explosive. It was discovered that she had a schizophrenic personality. When I first saw her, the old Adam in me became very angry, and I asked myself, "Why are they always bringing people with this kind of illness to me? By now they should know that I cannot offer much help." However, God's graciousness touched my heart, and I understood that, in the presence of this woman, Jesus Christ was meeting me and testing my understanding of his words: "Just as you did it to one of the least of these who are members of my family, you did it for me" (Matthew 25:40). In that revelatory moment, I made up my mind to respect, honor, and love that sick woman, who became for me the visible presence of the suffering Christ at my doorstep. Feeling loved and revered, Lina readily trusted and cooperated with me. In spite of a psychochirurgy that normally destroys all kinds of initiative, she never missed an appointment, and in the ensuing sessions, looked upon me benevolently.

Though I have no degrees in psychotherapy, I have read extensively the works of the great therapists of this century, giving special attention to those schools of therapy that emphasize healing relationships. This kind of healing becomes truly effective only to the degree that one has a deep and abiding respect for the sick person. Still, this is not enough. Along with learning and doing that which therapists require, it is also necessary to draw upon the mission of Christ entrusted to us and its consequences: "Proclaim the good news, 'The kingdom of heaven has come near.' Cure the sick...cleanse the lepers" (Matthew 10:7-8; see also Luke 10:9).

Learning techniques is essential, but the mission of healing involves infinitely more than that. The priest must open himself to the depths of faith, and with a heart full of gratitude and joy, put himself entirely in the hands of God. Most especially, a spirit of gratitude is the channel that opens hearts and minds to the gracious gifts of God's healing and liberating love. Thus, the point of departure is not what should I *do*, but more fundamentally what should I *be and bring to my relationships with God and my neighbor.* Only if the priest has himself opened his heart to receive the overwhelming peace and grace of God can the goodness flowing from his relationships heal the dear neighbor, especially those who are physically and mentally ill. This is considerably different from the "charitable" image of priest remote from the patient who benevolently looks "down from above" on his priestly perch.

Redemption, health, and healing are deeply marked by what theology calls *gratia praeveniens*. In explaining it to myself and to others, I liken it to a gracious gift given in advance. For example, it is always God who takes the initiative to trust and love us well in advance of anything we are, say, and do. Priests and ministers to the sick can enter fully into this economy of salvation to the extent that, in honoring God, they always offer the dear neighbor, even the most hostile, a prior and unconditional trust flowing from their goodness. The art of offering encouragement in advance is at the very heart of the biblical *Paraklesis*, the encouragement flowing from the power of the Spirit.

Young people who are routinely degraded, insulted, and blamed by parents and educators will inadvertently come to see themselves as worthless. "Dis-ease" with themselves early on can later lead to the development of paralyzed, sick, and lame adults, our modern-day lepers. Whereas parents and educators who live fully on the level of *Paraklesis* and wisely choose to trust children at the outset have the capacity to perform, in the true biblical sense, miracles that heal hearts and relationships first and foremost. Moreover, on that basis, they can at times even heal presenting illnesses themselves. These are the truly creative and therapeutic healers.

As priests, we should never attribute any kind of miraculous powers to ourselves by virtue of ordination. There is nothing miraculous or magical about us. On the other hand, God does great things in and through those who, like Mary, live a life of praise and abiding trust. True to our calling, we are nothing more and nothing less than humble coworkers with God who are open to receive God's graciousness to effect healing in all our relationships with God, others, and all of creation. The starting point is always our own realization that we, too, are in constant need of healing; we, too, are in need of the ongoing advance of God's gracious encouraging love and presence. At our very best, we are nothing short of wounded healers. In the measure that we unflinchingly encourage and trust others, this trust and encouragement flows back to us as healing and strengthening power.

Finally, it is not only the individual Christian, trained lay chaplain, and priest who are called and sent as ministers of healing. It is, above all, in the words of Teilhard de Chardin, the "Divine Milieu" from which all healing power derives and reaches out. This critical insight therefore obliges us to look for healthy relationships and healthy structures everywhere, within and beyond the Church. Moreover, this view arises from our fundamental mission to proclaim the Good News and to heal the sick in an integrated way.

## The Healing Task of Moral Theology and Moral Teaching

Only gradually did I discover that moral theology and, more generally, moral pedagogy have remarkable therapeutic and dynamic dimensions. One of the most important responsibilities is to help the Church, especially priests, to increasingly become mirror images, living symbols, of the great Healer, Jesus Christ, in living out the Gospel of healing. While priests have no monopoly on the Church's mission of healing and revelation, nonetheless, they best serve the people of God in pioneering and living an integrated model of the mission of healing, community-building, proclaiming, and witnessing to the Gospel.

It is always shocking to find within the Church a disturbing moralism that causes illness, anguish, scrupulosity, and aggression. Should ecclesiogenic pathologies that disturb nearly every essential relationship with God, self, and others exist, it is imperative that there be a concerted effort to scrutinize and amend all disciplines of theology, especially moral theology, which fail to synthesize and integrate the dimensions of healing and revelation. Of necessity, this task also calls for a reform of oppressive Church structures, such as those that foster bureaucratic centralism and an authoritarian view of leadership at all levels. In this endeavor, the starting point for reform must always be our collaborative efforts at wholly knowing Christ the Healer, Prophet, and the Incarnated image of the Creator.

Many Catholics were awakened by Karl Rahner's timely and fitting remark that, unfortunately, the Church, prior to the Council, declared trifles and bagatelles to be mortal sins. As a young moral theologian, I once preached a retreat in Tyrol for a hundred priests. In my introductory remarks, I said, "I do not intend to preach about a catalog of mortal sins." An old dean publicly reacted to my initial words by saying, "But this is not realistic! How could we priests avoid the possibility of mortal sin in relation to the rubrics?" His view of sin stemmed from the timeworn manual of Noldin, which outlined the numerous and required ritual prescriptions that priests were obliged to respect "under pain of mortal sin." For example, as late as 1949, the Vatican Congregation for Divine Worship and the Discipline of the Sacraments stated that a woman or a sister who, during Mass, approaches the altar beyond the communion rail is guilty of mortal sin. Some thirty years later, I found myself in conflict with a cardinal who enforced a particular Church law by obliging children over seven years of age to make first confession prior to receiving the Eucharist, since it was presumed that children at this age were capable of mortal sin.

That experience vividly reminded me of the horrors of my childhood experiences with my pastor who insisted we confess all our mortal sins, threatening us with fire and brimstone should our confessions be incomplete. What an image of God to present to children, not to mention adults! Thankfully, I did not then, nor do I now, share the pessimism of Eugen Drewermann, but even in this age, it is imperative that Church authorities, at every level, take into account the serious warnings of dedicated and knowledgeable psychotherapists who alert us to ecclesiogenic illness that can result from such a negative, erroneous, and punitive outlook.

It cannot be stressed enough that Church teaching and pastoral practice, in relation to all of life's dimensions and structures, must be liberated from a moral rigidity and reformulated within the perspective of a solid and humane synthesis of the twin ministries of proclamation and healing. Moreover, this synthesis must characterize priestly formation and life. While I have been, from the outset, a strong advocate of liberation theology, I firmly uphold the necessity of including the therapeutic dimension of liberation in all disciplines of theology.

## Pastoral Concern for the Divorced

My personal concern for people who are divorced did not arise from theoretical research, although I consider it very important. My interest stems from two main sources, namely, Jesus' loving compassion and respect for people on the margins of life—those who were considered as failures—and the richness of my own experience with people who are divorced.

The utter frustration and emotional suffering of so many divorced people should be sufficient reason not only to mobilize priestly compassion but also to lead the Church to a new kind of reflection. Almost everywhere in the world where I have served, my friends, especially religious men and women, have sent divorced people to me, or have addressed to me their concerns about divorced people they know. I can recall on one occasion when an African bishop sent his own divorced brother, a man of considerable stature, to me. The bishop said to his brother, "Do what Father Häring advises you to do!"

Time and again, the immense suffering of the divorced, most often admirable people, made me ponder and reflect upon Christ's words: "Just as you did it to one of the least of these who are members of my family, you did to me" (Matthew 25:40).

I am also deeply touched by Jesus' kindness toward the woman of Samaria who, in her quest for a decent life, had been abandoned by five men. In the Jewish tradition of that time, a "man of honor" would not even speak to such a woman. Jesus not only restored her sense of honor and dignity but, even more, he made her his apostle. As a disciple of Christ, I cannot even think of these needful people without hearing Jesus say: "I have not come to judge, but to heal" (see John 3:17; Luke 19:10).

In most of the cases of divorce brought to me, it has been more a question of tragic suffering and loss than of sin. On the basis of my experience and reflection, I increasingly became convinced that the therapeutic approach of the Orthodox *oikonomia* is much more congenial to Scripture than is the juridical ontologism of modern Catholicism. In my view, it is worth risking and accepting suffering in the forms of misunderstanding and criticism in an effort to reimagine and reformulate pastoral care aimed at healing these suffering and wounded people. As ministers of Christ to all his people, could we not fearfully imagine that Jesus could just as easily have written our names, yours and mine, in the dust and could as well have said to us: "Let anyone among you who is without sin be the first to throw a stone at her" (John 8:7-8)? Furthermore, many of the divorced who came to me can by no means be called adulterers.

The authentic priest is neither a judge nor a robot imprisoned in simplistic judgmental categories. Personally, I would be ashamed of myself if I felt even the slightest temptation to judge divorced and remarried people as "living objectively in a state of grave sin" after they have suffered so much pain and humiliation in the total breakdown of their first marriage.

Healing care for people who are divorced is also a test of the Church's commitment to the spirit of ecumenism. Orthodox Christians and many reformed Christians are shocked by the harshness of those Catholic priests and bishops who strictly adhere to an outdated juridical ontologism that undercuts, misunderstands, or totally replaces the biblical vision of indissolubility with the dreadful syndrome of simplistic thinking and control.

## CHAPTER 2

# THE GLARING LIGHT OF SCRIPTURE

J esus, who calls himself the "Son of Man"—"one of us"—asks John, the son of a priest and prophet, to baptize him along with a crowd in the Jordan. This action is a moving symbol of his saving solidarity with sinners and their rescue from the solidarity of sin.

### *A Decisive Key to Understanding: Christ's Baptism*

This transition from destructive sin to saving solidarity is at its heart a key to understanding the meaning of conversion preached by John, a conversion that, in its fullness, is finally made possible by Christ our Savior. Yet the baptism of Christ is infinitely more than this wondrous transition from the solidarity of sin to salvation. It is a unique Trinitarian event pointing directly to the cross and Resurrection of Christ. In his public baptism, Jesus consecrates himself and, at the same time, is consecrated by the power of the Spirit, symbolized by the dove of peace, in honor of his Father who gives testimony to Jesus forever: "This is my Son, the Beloved, with whom I am well pleased" (Matthew 3:17); "You are my Son, the Beloved, with you I am well pleased" (Luke 3:22; Mark 1:11). These words solemnly repeated on Mount Tabor hearken back to the programmatic verse in the first of the four songs in Deutero-Isaiah (Isaiah 42:1).

This baptismal anointing, which always points to the climax of the cross and Resurrection, manifests Jesus' identity as Savior and as the new High Priest, developed in the post-Pauline Letter to the Hebrews. Conceived by the Virgin Mary through the guiding power of the Holy Spirit, Christ is revealed as the nonviolent, suffering, and liberating Servant-Son of God, the true symbol and embodiment of the Dove of peace. He is the unerring Way, the Truth of peace, and the totally new Life of peace wrought by liberating nonviolence, saving solidarity, and by his suffering.

Priests, and all those who belong to the priestly, prophetic, and royal-servant people of God, can never meditate enough on the four songs of the Servant, considered by Jesus to be his program for life and service and, therefore, also the plan for his followers.

## Zechariah, Priest and Prophet

The new covenant and its totally new vision of priesthood is already symbolized in Zechariah, the father of John the Baptist, who belonged to one of the highest ranks of the Levitic priesthood and who fulfills a time-honored service when God reveals his son's role to him: "He will be filled with the Holy Spirit. He will turn many of the people of Israel to the Lord their God....[H]e will turn...the disobedient to the wisdom of the righteous" (Luke 1:15-17). The message of the angel was one of gladness: "You will have joy and gladness, and many will rejoice at his birth" (Luke 1:14).

The newness of, and the circumstances surrounding, this message is so great for Zechariah to absorb that it renders him mute. His very muteness is itself a symbol of this tremendous change. Still, he faithfully brings the news to his wife, Elizabeth, a descendant of the priestly line of Aaron and a woman of deep faith and prophetic vision.

The house of Zechariah becomes the privileged setting for a uniquely prophetic event. The whole household prophesies—Elizabeth, Zechariah, Mary—the humble handmaid of the Lord—and last but not least, baby John, who "leapt for joy in the womb" (Luke 1:44).

### John the Baptist, Son of a Priest and Great Prophet

According to the law, John would have been a member of a Jewish high priestly class. Yet nothing at all is said about John fulfilling time-honored priestly functions. The particular baptism of John, as a sign of conversion, is liturgical in the best sense of the word, but it totally contradicts any kind of ritualism. His baptism foreshadows the profound mystery of Jesus' baptism and, through it, our own baptism, which signals our entrance into the New Covenant of salvation—a covenant characterized by Jesus' vocation and identity as the humble, suffering, nonviolent, and healing Servant-Son of God.

At the heart of John's baptism is Jesus, the "Son of Man," the absolute embodiment of saving-solidarity who ushers in the New Law that means above all: "Bear one another's burdens, and in this way you will fulfill the law of Christ" (Galatians 6:2). Living this law is not only the path to unlimited and ongoing saving-solidarity, but it is also the only way out of sin-solidarity. The New Covenant is at the heart of the profound mystery of Jesus' baptism and, consequently, our own.

### The Contrast: Priests of Kings

The cruel and merciless killing of the prophet John the Baptist at the king's command foretells Christ's crucifixion and death at the hands of the high priests and the representative of the mighty Roman Empire.

The twin fates of John and Jesus exemplify the systemic abuse of religion that benefits the powerful at the expense of the powerless and poor. This form of abuse is also one of the greatest temptations among priests of different religions and cultures. One passage concerning the priest Amaziah in the book of Amos will suffice to show this truth:

> Amaziah, the priest of Bethel, sent to King Jeroboam of Israel, saying, "Amos has conspired against you in the very center of the house of Israel; the land is not able to bear all his words. For thus Amos has said,
>     'Jeroboam shall die by the sword,
>     and Israel must go into exile
>     away from his land.'"
> And Amaziah said to Amos, "O seer, go, flee away to the land of Judah, earn your bread there, and prophesy there; but never again prophesy at Bethel, for it is the king's sanctuary, and it is a temple of the kingdom" (Amos 7:10-13).

Several volumes could be written on this singular theme of the relationship between priests and kings, but it is enough to admit that within the Catholic Church many of us have reason to be contrite for being too closely allied with oppressive civil power. In a general way, it is helpful to show how this unholy relationship developed.

In the first three centuries of the Church, bishops, in particular, faithfully followed in the footsteps of Christ. It was a foregone conclusion that to become a bishop, priest, deacon, or church elder meant the very real possibility of becoming a candidate for martyrdom. These elected fairly well understood their general and special calling, and they were open to the risky consequences of it in the light of Jesus' baptism in the Jordan, a baptism of water and blood.

In the fourth century when Constantine, a "convert" to the faith, was crowned emperor by the bishop of Rome, drastic changes took place. While it is true that the Church was freed from bloody persecution, it quickly became evident that she was also greatly hampered in her quest to follow in the footsteps of Jesus the Servant. Accommodation of, and subservience to, civil authority (which Jesus questioned, as seen in the temptation midrash, and which he demythologized in the totality of his life from his baptism to the cross), unfortunately became a reality in all parts of the Church. All too many bishops either succumbed or came close to the fate of becoming "priests of the king."

In the quest to promote the Church and her leaders as pillars and signs of the kingdom, emperors and kings built palaces for them, heavily burdened them with every manner of worldly privilege, bestowed upon them pretentious and overblown titles such as "Theologian of the Court," "Prince-Archbishop," "His Grace," "His Holiness," and "Honorary Prelate of His Holiness," to name but a few.

This strange phenomenon and radical turn of events, which have consequences even to this day, must be reflected on and re-thought in the light of Jesus' baptism of water and blood. How we choose to see and reflect on these historical events that shaped a particular authoritarian image of Church and leadership can greatly impact the nature and quality of our fundamental option as Christians and priests in this age.

In general, Jesus was not hostile to the Jewish priesthood of his heritage, nor was he against priests *per se*. His major conflicts were with the highest-ranking members of the priestly cult. Worthy of note, however, is the fact that Jesus never called himself or his disciples "priests"; nor did he speak about the institution of a "new priesthood." At least the oldest parts of the New Testament writings closest to Jesus' time never used the word "priest" in addressing Jesus or his apostles. Only in the very late Letter to the Hebrews, written when the Church had developed a degree of organization and structure, was this vocabulary introduced, and it was mainly for the purpose of presenting a sharp contrast to anything that smacked of a questionable relationship that could have led to clerics becoming "priests of the kings." By contrast, the New Testament vision of priesthood is uniquely different, and it is especially made so in the light of Jesus' baptism of water in the Jordan and in his blood in the crucifixion.

### The Story of the Sacrifice of Abraham

It is not sufficient to merely elaborate on the glaring differences between the priesthood of the Old Testament and the newness of the servants of the Gospel. We must also caution against false concepts of sacrifice.

At times, theologians who have spoken on the idea of sacrifice chose as their starting point the willingness of Abraham to kill his son Isaac as a sacrificial offering of atonement to God. When I first studied theology, the belief that God tested Abraham's willingness to kill Isaac as a sacrificial offering was still being taught. That Abraham was *willing* is true, but that God *wanted this* is indeed highly suspect. In understanding the New Covenant priesthood, the first step in dispelling false notions of sacrifice is to understand the real meaning of the story of Abraham. To that end, some fifty years ago the noted biblical scholar W. Eichrodt offered quite a different explanation, which is commonly accepted in the biblical community and taught in catechetical circles today.

Eichrodt points out that, in the environment and primitive culture from which Abraham came and left for God's sake, there was a common conviction that, under certain circumstances, God could be placated only by the sacrifice of the firstborn son. It makes one wonder and shudder at how many firstborn sons throughout history were cruelly killed "in the name of God." Abraham was not yet free of this insidious superstition. Because he lived under circumstances in which, according to the tradition of his time, such a sacrifice was expected, Abraham, therefore, with erroneous conscience concluded that killing his son and offering him as sacrifice was the right thing to do. Yet, even in his erroneous conscience, something good can be said about Abraham: he was willing to do God's will as he falsely understood it. However, as the story develops, God intervened and liberated Abraham from a superstitious conscience. This was a tremendous revelatory experience and cultural breakthrough in the cause of liberating people from a terribly false and violent image of God.

One of the clearest proofs for Eichrodt's explanation is the well-established fact that, from that point on, there developed in Israel's consciousness a growing awareness that attempting to placate God with human sacrifice was an abominable crime of utter depravity against God and humankind. However, Scripture is also quick to point out that, in certain cruel periods of Israel's history, there were still some who were influenced and contaminated by this horrible view—a view that was also very much alive in the world surrounding Israel.

This false image of a vengeful God calling for human sacrifice of firstborn sons curiously enough found its way back into a theory of atonement attributed (perhaps falsely) to Saint Anselm. This led to the common misunderstanding that humankind's sinfulness was so great that God's justice required the sacrifice of his only begotten Son for atonement. Of course, this theory subsequently cast its dark shadow on almost everything considered to be sacrifice in relationship to Jesus himself. Nothing helps us more to clarify this misunderstanding than taking a closer look at the baptism of Jesus and all that follows in that light.

## The Nonviolent, Suffering, Liberating Servant of God

Mark's Gospel elucidates Jesus' identity and mission in the light of a central understanding found in the four servant-songs of Deutero-Isaiah: "For the Son of Man came not to be served but to serve" (Mark 10:45). As the Servant, Jesus is acknowledged as beloved Son. In the Hebrew text, the programmatic first verse speaks of *ebed*, which means the honored servant to whom everything can be entrusted. The Septuagint uses the Greek term *pais* for son. In light of the servant-songs, Jesus is understood above all as the servant of peace—an understanding that in no way encompasses any false notion of God's need for appeasement. Rather, *it is for humankind to find the way of peace* in Jesus himself, who is the way of peace and the embodiment of nonviolence.

Jesus' call to love one's enemies is the way that transforms the enemy into a friend. The way of peace Jesus shows us is one of nonviolence that prefers suffering and even death over killing or harming the enemy. It is precisely the liberating force of nonviolence that underpins a profound and total readiness *to clear the way for peace,* and to do so in a life-giving manner. Jesus is the Truth, and in a very specific way, he is the Truth of liberating nonviolence.

But the question remains: Did God want the sacrifice of his only Son? Because we stand before a profound mystery and because, from our side of things, we can only speak within the limits of our human language, perspective, and context, which are always partial and incomplete, the answer is both yes and no. In the dynamic interrelationship of the Trinity, God wanted to show humankind the way of peace *whatever the cost.* Thus, the "sacrifice of Christ" is both the death-dealing and life-giving price of peace and reconciliation, the ultimate price of the unique revelation of God's infinite love. But, in understanding this cost, a word of caution is necessary. In no way did God intend or plan the murder of Jesus, the beloved Son. What God truly envisioned was the reconciliation of a peaceful, nonviolent humanity. Moreover, God wanted, and continues to want, our willingness to pay the price of peace, reconciliation, and ongoing redemptive love as understood in Paul's words: "He [Jesus] is our peace" (Ephesians 2:14).

To make it as clear as possible, the Trinity of Creator, Redeemer, and Creative Unifier forbids killing and, in a very particular way, forbids any killing in the name of God. To do so is the most abominable crime. Consequently, what this understanding clarifies for all time is that God never intended that the Son Incarnate be killed as a victim of divine appeasement or atonement.

What was truly intended was the willingness to take the supreme risk even of death on a cross should that be necessary to reveal God's infinite love and to show humankind the way of peace, truth, and life. Ultimately, this was the price Christ paid, even to the point of praying on the cross for his enemies and all sinners alike. Thus, the killing of Jesus on the cross was the *consequence* of that risk and *not* the "agreeable sacrifice" that, having been taught for centuries, unwittingly promoted an image of a cruel and vindictive God.

All three Synoptic gospels present the story of Jesus' baptism in the light of the four servant-songs. Even the Gospel of John explicitly makes the point: "Here is the Lamb of God who takes away the sin of the world!" (John 1:29). John also reminds us of the central theme of the first and fourth servant-songs: "He will not cry or lift up his voice, / or make it heard in the streets; / a bruised reed he will not break, / and a dimly burning wick he will not quench" (Isaiah 42:2-3); "He was oppressed, and he was afflicted, / yet he did not open his mouth; / like a lamb that is led to the slaughter, / and like a sheep that before its shearers is silent, / so he did not open his mouth" (Isaiah 53:7).

An awful consequence of such flawed thinking that would make Jesus a scapegoat is the English text of *The Jerusalem Bible* which still clings to the translation: "Yahweh has been pleased to crush him with suffering" (Isaiah 53:10). Can we say that God found pleasure in crushing Jesus? *The New English Bible* and all the new ecumenical translations say something quite different: "Yet the Lord took thought for his tortured Servant and healed him who made himself a sacrifice" (Isaiah 53:10).

While we can and will continue to speak of "sacrifice" as a way of liberation from sin-solidarity to the solidarity of peace, unselfish love, and saving justice, sacrifice rightly understood implies hard choices with difficult consequences for priests and Christians. There can be no escape into ritualism, no bloody asceticism, and no "mere" sacrifice outside the true understanding of the history of life. Moreover, all of us must be ready and eager to give up what hinders us on the path of peace and justice toward God, and we must be willing to shoulder the burdensome demands of peace and reconciliation by taking on the risk of suffering, even unto death, should it be required by the Gospel of peace—the Gospel of the suffering Servant of God.

It cannot be emphasized enough that God, whom we call Father and Mother of our Savior Jesus Christ, does not want and does not allow any kind of sacrifice that leads us to escape our true calling in and for the history of salvation. The real meaning of Christ's sacrifice demands, without question, a spirit of personal sacrifice, an absolute readiness to take upon ourselves the burdens of our sisters and brothers, and an unflinching courage to face conflict, suffering, and risk—all of which can arise in promoting peace, justice, and redemptive love.

### Nonviolence and the Forgiveness of Sin

The centrality of Christ's self-understanding as the nonviolent Servant and Sacrament of Peace also sheds light on the present crisis surrounding the sacrament of reconciliation.

The great midrash on the Flood symbolizes, in a drastic way, the dangerous path to self-destruction of the entire human race through violence and falsehood, both of which always go hand in hand with pride and arrogance. "Now the earth was corrupt in God's sight, and the earth was filled with violence. And God saw that the earth was corrupt; for all flesh had corrupted its ways upon the earth" (Genesis 6:11-12).

The Bible speaks of a long history of patriarchal violence. Lamech, who threatens his wives and who is a descendant of the murderous Cain, is a striking example of this truth: "You wives of Lamech, listen to what I say: / 'I have killed a man for wounding me, / a young man for striking me. / If Cain is avenged sevenfold, / truly Lamech seventy-sevenfold'" (Genesis 4:23-24).

What is clear is that only nonviolent people will be saved in and through the Flood. Jesus himself refers to this vision when Peter asks: "'Lord, if another member of the church sins against me, how often should I forgive? As many as seven times?' Jesus said to him, 'Not seven times, but, I tell you, seventy-seven times'" (Matthew 18:21-22). Matthew's adaptation of this curious metaphor illustrates Jesus' overwhelming desire that we forgive endlessly.

While being baptized with Christ "for the forgiveness of sins" means being pardoned, it means ever so much more in that all are rescued from the fate of sin-solidarity, all are brought home to saving solidarity, and all are invited to be coworkers in Christ's earthly mission of peace and reconciliation.

If the ministerial priesthood can be said to add something to the universal priesthood of all the baptized, it surely means that priests must be, at all levels, models of forgiveness, leaders, and peacemakers on the road to healing nonviolence and reconciliation. Implied is a self-emptying quality and an openness to a proper understanding of self-denial. In other words, priests must be peacemakers who refuse no risk, no burden, and no proper sacrifice deemed necessary in promoting the mission of Christ. Openness and self-denial presume a humble willingness to collaborate with people of goodwill for the sake of human redemption from sin-solidarity in all of its unjust, fallacious, and violent forms, wherever they be found. This is radically different from self-defeating and highly questionable ascetical practices that, among others, include self-affliction and needless suffering for some specious purpose of softening the wrath of a wrongly perceived vengeful God.

The Letter to the Hebrews points to Christ as the compassionate high priest, and it is precisely this compassionate and loving attitude that motivates Christ to be merciful to sinners. What characterizes the true priest is that "He is able to deal gently with the ignorant and wayward, since he himself is subject to weakness;

and because of this he must offer sacrifice for his own sins as well as for those of the people" (Hebrews 5:2-3).

I have a healing and comforting proposal for priests and Christians alike who anguish over whether or not they have rightly confessed all grave sins, all accurately numbered and classified by category and species, and it is this: Concentrate all your attention and energies on becoming, as it were, a kind of sacrament, a visible and convincing sign of healing, forgiveness, and nonviolence as much as is possible! Then you can be assured in faith that God forgives you and all your sins. It is only in purposefully taking this route that we can contribute to overcoming the present crisis surrounding the sacrament of peace and reconciliation.

## The Priesthood of the Faithful and the Ministerial Priesthood

The Second Vatican Council made great strides in overcoming the age-old structural sin of clericalism, which, among other things, tended to distinguish priests from laity in dualistic terms of superiority and inferiority and which, consequently, led to many forms of distance and alienation in the Church. From a liturgical standpoint, those barriers were never made more clear to me than several years ago when I visited a number of churches in Italy where the altar was situated one floor above the nave. At that time, it was rare for a priest to step down into the body of the Church, even at Communion time.

Thankfully, the decision of the Council to entrust all baptized, nonordained Christians with important pastoral and liturgical roles was a major step in breaking down those barriers. Most of us know by now that the priesthood is not at all a step upward on the social ladder, but rather a particular commitment to descend, in humility and service, to where the people are, so as to be "one among them." In so doing, the significance of the priesthood has not been lost. Rather, in that sense, the priesthood has been wholly restored, strengthened, and deepened in its redirection to Christ's humble baptism among the many, as a sign of his identity as the wholesome High Priest. Universal and ministerial priesthood point *together* to our baptismal call to service on behalf of Messianic peace on this earth.

## CHAPTER 3

# REACHING FOR THE DEEPER MEANING AND PURPOSE OF THE PRIESTLY VOCATION

The special calling of Matthew (Levi) is a splendid example of the free gift of vocation to laity and clergy alike. As Jesus was walking along, he saw a man called Matthew sitting at the tax booth; and he said to him, "Follow me." And he got up and followed him. And as he sat at dinner in the house, many tax collectors and sinners came and were sitting with him and his disciples (Matthew 9:9-10).

### The Calling of Levi
### and the Messianic Meal

Levi is a true religious genius in that he realizes and expresses this gratuity in a creative way from the very beginning: "If the Master invites me, an old swindler, a despised tax collector, why should he then not welcome my old friends?" That same day, Levi prepares a meal for Jesus and people like himself. Could he have realized his gesture was symbolic of the Messianic meal and of the newness of the kingdom of heaven? For us, Levi's gesture should be a very convincing expression of the meaning of our own vocation.

Levi's hospitality, which broke down human barriers and all pretense of superiority, did not go unnoticed by the Pharisees, who asked Jesus' disciples, "Why does your teacher eat with tax collectors and sinners?" (Matthew 9:11). In parallel fashion, our whole history of exclusive admission to the Eucharist is evidenced in the Pharisees' question born of an attitude of exclusivity. The centrality of Jesus' mercy and compassionate healing love in this scene are summed up in his challenging response: "Those who are well have no need of a physician, but those who are sick. Go and learn what this means, 'I desire mercy, not sacrifice.' For I have come to call not the righteous but sinners" (Matthew 9:12-13).

Perhaps there will always be a particular class of priests who will fail to learn and embody the core vision of Jesus' healing compassion and humility, and who will instead promote an erroneous view of "sacrifice." Yet, like Matthew, true priests cannot find genuine happiness in the company of Jesus by categorically excluding any person from the Messianic meal with the argument: "They are objectively in the state of mortal sin."

On this matter, as in others, those who truly live a religious life exude deep awe, wonderment, and an inner "knowing" of the gratuitous heart of Christ that enable them to break down all human barriers in opposition to self-righteousness. Of course, these qualities also include a capacity for a distinctively Christian discernment that, first of all, should make all us priests fearful of being excluded ourselves from the bliss of the Messianic meal in view of our own self-righteousness and lack of compassion. We had best never think or speak of others as sinners before first confessing that we, too, are poor sinners. In this context, should priests always try to give the impression of being holy men, or at least of being men without fault? Clearly, this question needs probing.

The Polish writer Mary Winowska tells a moving story of a priest who, in the eyes of his parishioners, truly appeared to be a faultless man. One day, the secret police of the Gestapo came to him and, after a brief introduction, said to the surprised pastor, "We feel sure that you will be willing to cooperate with us by giving us all the necessary information about the Church since you enjoy the trust of the bishops and priests." The pastor replied, "God forbid, no!" Then the police showed him a picture of a woman and her child and asked, "Are you not the father of this child?"

In view of the evidence, the pastor asked for time to reflect until Sunday of that week. At the Sunday Mass, something new and different transpired. In place of the ritual Confiteor, the pastor chose to confess all his serious sins, including those not known by the Gestapo, before the entire community, in which sat two members of the secret police. He asked their forgiveness and their blessing to go elsewhere and do penance. The reaction of the parishioners was overwhelming. They wept with him and asked aloud that he remain. Because of his public confession, the faithful loved him even more, for now he had manifested himself as "one of us" in his sinfulness.

To answer the original question, without a doubt the priest must thoroughly know he is called to holiness to the point of becoming a source of encouragement and inspiration to all on the road to Christian wholeness. However, any false appearance of holiness would be a major deterrent to that quest. A priest who cannot acknowledge that he, too, lives by God's forgiveness and that he, too, errs has no credibility whatsoever.

It would do well for us to choose Levi-Matthew as a patron. In so doing, we might find ourselves to be more effective priests, insofar as we are more readily open to inviting outsiders to Jesus' Messianic meal and, in so doing, find ourselves more welcomed by him. As with Levi, we need to deeply understand and actualize the words of Jesus: "I came not to judge the world, but to save the world" (John 12:47).

The more we humbly praise God's healing love for all men and women, the more we can become, through God's grace, effective "wounded healers." For certain, priests should never consider any people under their care as "hopeless cases." All our pastoral sensitivities and conduct should be impregnated by a growing awareness of God's undeserved and unlimited advance of love even as we reflect on our own experience of need. At best, all we can do is remain open to God's generous disposition and, in recognizing it, personify God's generosity in our pastoral attitude and untiring practice of encouraging others. Let Levi be our guide!

## The Washing of Feet at the Last Supper

Jesus' baptism in the Jordan and his washing of the feet of the apostles at the last supper complete each other. In raising foot-washing to the level of ritual, Jesus symbolizes his freely accepted baptism in his own blood for the remission of sin and for the victory of nonviolent love. In choosing this service, usually attributed to the lowest class of servants, Jesus leaves no doubt that this humble gesture, which sheds light on the totality of his life and death, should be considered the highest norm, especially for those called to share in his mission of proclaiming the Good News and of uniting all disciples in his love.

Although John's Gospel is, in a very prominent way, a eucharistic Gospel, it provides no explicit account of the institution of the Eucharist. As with numerous biblical scholars, I consider the account of the washing of the feet in its context to be a wonderful eucharistic text. It is indeed an indispensable key to a deeper understanding of both the Eucharist and the priesthood.

After washing the feet of his disciples, Jesus reveals to us his unique relationship with his Father. Moreover, he reveals who *Abba* is to us in this ritual washing, in his self-offering as the bread of life, and finally, in the shedding of his life-giving blood. John highlights this revelation in the prayer of Jesus: "Father, the hour has come; glorify your Son so that the Son may glorify you, since you have given him authority over all people, to give eternal life to all whom you have given him. And this is eternal life, that they may know you, the only true God, and Jesus Christ whom you have sent" (John 17:1-3).

There are some who passionately oppose the ordination of women on the supposition that women were not present at the Last Supper and, therefore, they conclude that the New Testament priesthood is unquestioningly a male prerogative. Perhaps women were not present, but we can only speculate here. More important is the fact that women were present to Jesus, actively involved in his life ministry, and continued to be so in significant and priestly ways in the budding Church.

Not only did women accompany Jesus as humble servants, but they faithfully remained at the foot of the cross when others left. A woman was the first to see the risen Lord in the Easter event and to spread that good news—the selfsame event we celebrate worthily in the Eucharist only when we deny all claims of superiority and make ourselves, with these women, servants of the Servant of Yahweh.

John, the beloved disciple and faithful friend of Peter, makes it clear how difficult it was for Peter to allow himself to enter into the heart of the mystery of Christ in the washing of the feet. Of course, this ritual is meaningless to anyone who cannot accept it as a fundamental rule of the Christian life and, in a particular way, of priestly apostolic ministry. When Peter asked if Jesus was going to wash his feet, Jesus answered, "You do not know now what I am doing, but later you will understand." Shocked, Peter said, "You will never wash my feet." Then Jesus said, "Unless I wash you, you have no share with me" (see John 13:7-8). It is only with this ultimatum that Peter gives in, though he does not realize the full extent of its meaning for him. Like Peter, we, too, are only dimly aware of its import on our journey toward a fuller existential understanding.

In part, the cause of Peter's troubled spirit and that of others is due largely to a mistaken image of the Messiah prevalent at that time. In Jesus' time, the *anawim,* the poor and humble Israelites, such as Mary and Joseph, wholeheartedly sang and proclaimed the servant-songs. In contrast to their hope, however, there prevailed among the influential elite an expectation of a powerful national liberator who would free Israel from Roman oppression.

When we ponder Mark's Gospel, it is astounding at first to read that on different occasions Jesus is portrayed as one who asks the apostles not to disclose him as the Messiah. In the Marcan drama, this is done for good reason. Since Peter and the followers of Christ held strong attachments to a power-Messiah, it would have been impossible for them at that point to give credence to the Son of Man, "one of us," as the Messiah. It was only when the apostles became thoroughly disenchanted with this notion of power they could, with deep faith in the Servant of God, come to understand him as the true, empowering Messiah.

In applying this truth to myself, I come to see that it is only to the extent that I "know" the Servant of God, the Son of Man, and only in the totality of my person and conduct as a servant of the Servant, can there be any meaning in praising Jesus as the Messiah. To the extent that any priest, deacon, or pastorally trained person clings to worldly privilege, titles, and honors, or maintains an air of false superiority, everything that can be said about the "dignity" of the ordained priesthood and the priesthood of the people becomes insipid, misleading, and totally false.

In every era, God has sent truly prophetic priests to the Church and the world who, having been marked by deep humility and clairvoyance, focused their hearts and minds on the baptism of the Servant of Yahweh, on the Son of Man's washing the feet of his disciples, on his preeminent power of love for the most poor and powerless on this earth, and finally on his willingness to embrace the cross. And all of these focal points are celebrated in the action of the eucharistic meal where the risen Christ is deeply present.

## *The Folly of Disputes Over Preeminence*

If we have not fully unmasked our personal tendencies for honor-seeking and all forms of self-exaltation, we should be shocked into reality when reading the scriptural account of the tenacity with which the apostles argued among themselves as to who should be the greatest. It seems totally incredible that, immediately after Jesus had washed the feet of his disciples and had explained its profound meaning, we should read:

> A dispute also arose among them as to which one of them was to be regarded as the greatest. But he said to them, "The kings of the Gentiles lord it over them; and those in authority over them are called benefactors. But not so with you; rather the greatest among you must become like the youngest, and the leader like one who serves. For who is greater, the one who is at the table or the one who serves? (Luke 22:24-27).

Nor should we be surprised to know that it was not beyond James and John to bid directly with Jesus and through their own mother for places of honor at his side. Could they not have seen how such an ignoble request might have hurt Jesus? In reply, Jesus said, "You do not know what you are asking. Are you able to drink the cup that I drink, or be baptized with the baptism that I am baptized with?" (Mark 10:38).

This text is important to us because it is precisely here that Jesus asks us to understand our own baptism in relation to his baptism as the nonviolent Servant—a baptism of blood. The critical insight here for Christians and especially for priests is that everything is at stake. Either we take the fundamental option to follow the Servant-Messiah faithfully, humbly, and courageously, even to the point of suffering unto death if need be, or we remain slaves to alienation and pride.

Mark 9:30-37 is a literary and pedagogical masterpiece. Mark has Jesus present his core message to his apostles: "The Son of

Man is to be betrayed into human hands, and they will kill him, and three days after being killed, he will rise again" (Mark 9:31).

Jesus then goes ahead of them toward the fulfillment of what he has just explained. On the road, the apostles kept their distance so that Jesus would not hear what they were saying. But he knows. Once gathered in the house at Capernaum, Jesus asked, "What were you arguing about on the way?" They are silent because the subject of their conversation centered around who was the greatest among them. Might they have had a bad conscience and therefore wished that Jesus, having just revealed his terrible fate, not know what was on their minds?

Have we become any wiser after twenty centuries of Church history? If we are honest, even the best among us will admit they find themselves at times in tempting situations that invite self-promotion. At the Second Vatican Council, warnings against Church triumphalism were frequently sounded. At the very last session, several cardinals, patriarchs, bishops, and some theologians, including myself, were gathered to discuss a final proposal to the Council, and it was this: We had planned that the Council Fathers should not return to their respective dioceses without first having solemnly pledged apostolic poverty and, above all, apostolic simplicity by renouncing all antievangelical titles such as "Honorary Prelate to His Holiness"—a title still greatly desired today. Several hundred bishops were ready for this step. However, time was pressing, and the proposal never came to pass. It is my conviction that we could have spared the Church many troubles after the Council had we adopted and faithfully observed a clear and official decision on this matter.

With unsurpassable clarity, the temptation midrash (Matthew 4:1-11) totally unmasks the satanic temptations to use religion for the sake of utility, self-exaltation, and earthly power; and it reveals these temptations to be in direct opposition to the vocation of the Servant-Messiah. These horrific temptations are a thousand times more dangerous than, for example, masturbation, premarital sex, contraception, and other sexual concerns that the Church so frequently discusses and inculcates in the minds of the faithful.

Alienation of religion and, above all, degradation of the full revelation of Jesus, the Servant of God, through human pride, arrogance, and the lust for power are truly diabolic. We can never do too much when it comes to unmasking these seductions—first of all in ourselves and then in the larger Church and in the world. The radical work of exposing these temptations for what they are is only possible to the degree that our hearts and minds are fixed on Jesus, the Servant of Yahweh.

### Jesus the Carpenter

In the economy of salvation, Jesus, from the outset, was to be born and grow up in the milieu of the poor. Called "son of the carpenter" or simply "the carpenter," he was used to hard work, and with any degree of imagination, we can visualize him happily working for people, helping them build their homes. The image of Jesus the worker fits neatly into the larger image of Jesus, the Servant of Yahweh, the Son of Man. Last but not least, it ties well into the central picture of Jesus' baptism in the Jordan amid the gathering of ordinary people who had accepted John's preaching of conversion.

I can recall in the late fifties how shocked many of us were when Cardinal Giuseppe Pizzardo, the powerful head of the Holy Office, banned the initiatives of worker priests with the strange argument that the position of a dependent worker contradicts the dignity of the priesthood. Of course this movement did contradict his view of the priesthood, garnered from the whole history of career-dreaming priests who were focused, from the start, on ecclesial titles and privileges that could lead them all the way to the cardinal's hat. The worker-priest concept must have petrified these career-minded clerics striving for trappings and bagatelles that were more vain and more ridiculous than even those of the mighty of this world.

Ironically, as I write these very lines, an anonymous letter has just arrived with this injunction: "Stop criticizing the Church! You, too, could be clothed in purple." Of significance is the sad reality that this writer symbolizes the connection between blind obedience and the drivenness to honors that once characterized and still motivates ecclesiastical careerists today. It is in glaring contrast to Jesus the carpenter and his apostles, who were mainly fishermen. Even Paul, the tentmaker, continued his work alongside his full-time apostolic responsibilities as did the dear doctor, Luke, who maintained his healing activities when he was Paul's companion in the ministry of evangelization.

As we consider God's plan of salvation, we find that the Incarnation of the Word of God into poverty, into the social milieu of the poor and lower class, is a glaring contradiction to all forms of self-promotion. More than all the prophets before him, in tandem with his unique attachment to the "adoration of God in spirit and truth," Jesus denounced and exposed every misuse of religion for personal gain.

At this point, it is necessary to reemphasize the only name Jesus ever gave himself—"Son of Man" (ben adám). The Letter to the Hebrews clearly explains it in this way: "He had to become like his brothers and sisters in every respect, so that he might be a merciful and faithful high priest in the service of God" (2:17). A later verse says: "One who in every respect has been tested as we are, yet without sin" (4:15).

Wherever there exists in the Catholic faith or any Christian tradition an elite clerical caste molded by a system of privilege that separates them from ordinary people, such a sect becomes the tasteless salt of hypocrisy and a flagrant contradiction to the Gospel's maxim that urges us to be salt for the earth and the light of the world. Thus, in the glaring light of the Gospel, any distinction between clergy and laity based upon rank and privilege is utterly despicable.

In the very early Church, objection to military service became a distinctive sign for all Christian followers of the nonviolent

Servant. However, as the Church adjusted to the changes wrought by the Edict of Constantine in A.D. 313, a surprising new distinction appeared between priests (now indeed "clergy") and laity. Refusing military service based on nonviolence suddenly became a privilege for a certain class of people—namely, the clergy—while, at the same time, ordinary people were now expected to render military service should they be ordered to do so.

On one hand, priestly exemption appeared to have safeguarded the clerical role of giving witness to Christ the Peacemaker, the nonviolent Servant of Yahweh; but, on the other hand, priests and bishops allowed themselves to be used to reinforce the military service of "ordinary" Christians. Hereby, the whole meaning of being baptized in the name of Jesus, the nonviolent Savior, which characterized all the priestly people of God, was thoroughly perverted. How can I, as a priest, claim that my witness to, and identification with, Christ as Peacemaker forbids me to render military service if, at the same time, I as priest tell my fellow Christians that they must abide by a civil law that requires military service?

As a priest-medic in World War II, I profited from this exemption insofar as I could. Were there no exemption, I would have faced a serious moral crisis, for in conscience I could never have taken up arms in that insidious war. When I say I profited, I must point out that priestly exemption was a costly affair because, as it turned out, priest-medics had the highest death toll among the various military units. However, willingness to die unarmed in the service of life and healing is something strikingly different from a willingness to die while participating in the killing of other human beings. So, in that sense, I profited greatly. I might add that nearly every member of the Mennonite Peace Church in Germany categorically refused to participate in the military, and consequently many went to their death at the command of Hitler for their staunch witness to nonviolence.

For centuries leading up to our present time, many Catholic bishops and clergy on both sides of warring parties played a very sad and compliant role—a role that stressed obedience to Caesar when indeed obedience to Christ was called for. One example from this century will suffice. When the Austrian sacristan Jägerstatter refused military service "under such a criminal as Hitler," both his pastor and bishop tried to convince him that it would be better to accept conscription than to die. He, however, was wiser and braver than the clergy.

In the light of Christ's baptism, life, and death, I am convinced that profound dedication to nonviolence and peacemaking are constitutive to the Christian and priestly calling. In all professions and sectors of life, there is a need to give special attention to the promotion of a synthesis of justice, love, peace, and nonviolence.

I hesitate somewhat on the oft-asked question as to whether priests should take up political positions in an effort to promote peace, justice, nonviolence, and worldwide peace. Still, as priests and especially as theologians, we must do our best to promote vocations to the political life. On the other hand, priests who believe they must be present to, and active in, every arena of life signal the potential for failure in their vocation to preach and give witness to the centrality of what characterizes Jesus, the Servant of Yahweh.

Throughout Church history, Christian men and women, totally dedicated to Gospel values of peace and nonviolence, have ministered to the poor, the handicapped, the outcast, and the sick, in deeply pastoral and creative ways. With some imagination, could the Church not empower these ministers of Christ to exercise specific priestly functions heretofore only granted to the ordained? And should men and women be so authorized, as in the case of the restored diaconate (if still, unfortunately, a male prerogative), could they not also be granted ordination if they so desire?

### Witness to the Resurrection

Just prior to the election of Matthias to complete the apostolic circle, Peter provides an illuminating description of the requirements as recorded in Acts: "So one of the men who have accompanied us during all the time that the Lord Jesus went in and out among us, beginning from the baptism of John until the day when he was taken up from us—one of these must become a witness with us to his resurrection" (1:21-22).

I find it highly significant that Peter reminds the apostles of the importance of Jesus' baptism by John, because that extraordinary event revealed Jesus, as the nonviolent Servant of Yahweh, was pleased to take on our burdens. For all Christians and, with particular urgency, all bishops and priests, this mystery should serve as the template of their own witnessing to the humility and nonviolence of Jesus, as well as to his transformation of enemies into friends through unconditional love.

Familiarity with Jesus in the company of his disciples is a second requirement. This means knowing Christ as Son of God who was "Son of Man" and "one of us." Knowing Christ as Christ understood himself to be disposes us, like him, to set our eyes on the road to Jerusalem. Always looking forward to the things yet to be fulfilled in Jerusalem is how the Gospel writers interpret this requirement, and how they characterize the company of Jesus' apostles. It is a rough, unpolished road fraught with uncertainties and surprises.

Why is it that Peter does not explicitly mention to the soon-to-be-chosen apostle that someone must be present to the death of Christ on the cross? With the exception of John, this was a crucial point. Had Peter insisted that one of the elected would have to be a direct witness to Christ's suffering and death, the apostles might very well have proposed a woman in their ranks. For as the Gospels point out, there were many women who followed Jesus on the way to Calvary and stood by him to the end. Christians in all eras have honored these courageous and saintly women who, with Mary and John, were eyewitnesses to Jesus' death. Moreover, it was Mary Magdalene who was the first to witness the Resurrection and bring the good news to the apostles. Nonetheless, the newly chosen apostle was a male, because for the apostles, steeped as they were in their Jewish patriarchal heritage, the number twelve came to signify the twelve sons of Jacob. Hence, given that symbolic understanding, a male was chosen.

Even so, Peter's main emphasis is on witnessing to the Resurrection of the crucified Christ, the suffering Servant of Yahweh—a witnessing that is central to the Christian calling and deeply characteristic of those called to proclaim the Good News in a particular way. It is my hope that all who read this book will see everything else of which I speak in this light. I would point out here that priests who are not, in a very specific and convincing way, witnesses to the Resurrection of Christ and of all believers are sham representatives of Christ.

Since witnessing to the Resurrection of the suffering Servant is the nucleus of our ongoing examination of conscience and the test of priestly identity, the fundamental question always before us is this: whether or not we are prepared to wholeheartedly embody the suffering, compassionate, humble Servant in a spirit of joy that flows from our faith in Christ's and our own resurrection. Are people aware that it is our lived faith that is the source of our endurance, patience, and joy in the midst of affliction, illness, tension, and dissent? Reflection on the depth of our faith in the risen Christ, of necessity, turns our attention time and again to our own baptism in Christ, the humble, patient Servant of Yahweh.

## A Grateful Memory

At the heart of the new people of God in their earthly pilgrimage toward the end-time stands the Eucharist. The Eucharist is the grateful celebration of Jesus' baptism of water in the Spirit and baptism of fire in his suffering, passion, death, and Resurrection. It is a celebration of his exaltation as humble Servant in whom resides our own hope for eternal life. If the Christian life is to be understood and lived within the perspective of the history of God's salvific presence, then the eucharistic celebration is the summit of that presence—a summit whereby we encounter and become present to the Savior and Redeemer of human history.

Inserting our present moment and past history into the saving history of Christ becomes *kairos* time—a time of favor, a unique opportunity that links the past with the future. Celebration with a truly grateful memory makes whole again the wealth of God's saving deeds in history and links them to our own life-giving endeavors and failures. Our endeavors and failures receive their fullest meaning in that intersection with the Lord of history. Here, in this moment of the risen Christ's presence, we are offered his life-giving energies to continue our journey into the future with him—a future of anguish and joy that will call us to new challenges and responsibilities in our enduring hope and expectation of the final fulfillment on the Day of the Lord. It is indeed the hour of "already" meeting the Lord with whom we hope to celebrate the fullness of his victory—and ours—of love in the yet-to-come.

A truly grateful eucharistic memory fills us with joy and trust, and often arouses us to a greater sense of readiness and vigilance. The energies of a grateful memory empower us anew to continue on the road to Jerusalem, toward all of life's demands and difficulties without ever losing sight of the Resurrection. The fruitfulness of our present hour in the presence of the Lord of history stems as much from past energies kept alive in grateful memory as it does from our present hope that enlivens and deepens our sense of personal and corporate responsibility. Our fortitude and endurance are strengthened in the communion rite through which we are intimately incorporated into Christ, who was, who is, and who will ever be.

While all that is said about the Eucharist is true for every Christian, it raises crucial questions for humble presiders over the Word and the Eucharist. Are we increasingly becoming living signs of the dynamics of history in our priestly role? As servants of Christ, are we open to allowing the risen Christ to incorporate us more and more into the pilgrim community? Are we increasingly becoming attuned to the importance of collaboration and co-responsibility with the gathered faithful as concelebrants of our faith?

From what I have shared thus far, criteria for who should preside at the Eucharist necessarily emerges. It seems to me that each and all of the requirements of priestly life thus far discussed are far more weighty than the narrow and highly questionable biological issue of sex.

The Eucharist is the paschal hour, the movement and transition of the Lord. Is it a time of rest? It surely is, but even more it is the moment of new departure, an opportunity for human adventure far greater than what Moses and the Israelites experienced. In each Eucharistic celebration, it is Christ who invites us anew: "Get up, let us be going!" (Matthew 26:46).

That Christ does bid us rest does not imply we become "seated" persons. Who are they? To answer the question, it is important that we understand it in the light of our most fundamental query: what kind of priests does the Church require? Seated persons are those women and men who are forever tired, devoid of ideals and inspiration, who are unable to enlist the power of the Spirit to encourage others. The seated person is one who is incapable of interiorizing Jesus' invitation: "Up, let us go forward," most especially if going forward implies the risk of potential suffering, change, and temporary insecurity. The seated person is static and self-satisfied, ever content to celebrate past triumphs and achievements while ever avoiding the courageous responsibility that risktaking involves. In a word, the seated person is cowardly.

Ordinarily, the self-satisfied are fundamentalist in their thinking, eschewing new and creative formulations of doctrine while ever clinging to the norms and imperatives of the past. They are hard-and-fast traditionalists and, if gifted with energies, they use them strenuously to promote the restoration of a past order. Seated persons are those perched on self-made thrones unwilling to move forward with the times because such a move would mean renouncing the glamour and privilege of clericalism in all its forms at every level.

Our era of rapid change and new development reveals a unique problem. The Church of today suffers greatly because of those priests and bishops who, wedded to their various chairs, titles, and offices, encourage the faithful to turn back the clock, to look back to a timeworn era, but who are unaware that such a move would make us all, not unlike Lot's wife, into pillars of salt. Only if we are contemporary with Jesus, the Lord of history, the One who came, comes, and will come again, can we go forward together. Indeed, it is true that going forward with Jesus in grateful memory is, in the eyes of many, too dangerous a remembrance and challenge. If the risen Christ of history can choose to be wholly present to us in the action of breaking bread and sharing the cup, can he not also transform seated persons into untiring pilgrims and vanguards of history? Such would be a great and hoped-for miracle for which we should all pray.

Attempting to shape future history as nonviolent and courageous peacemakers is unequivocally the grand adventure of our times. If the grateful memory of the Sermon on the Mount could so impact men and women like Mahatma Gandhi, Martin Luther King, Jr., Dorothy Day, and the courageous foundresses of religious communities and transform them into imaginative pioneers and pilgrim people who are moving ever forward, why then are such leaders so rare today?

In this light, there is little doubt that we need a liturgical renewal, but we need one that far surpasses the current focus on ritual debate. From the outset, we need to become, in a radically transformed way, more faith-filled and hopeful people, with open ears, hearts, and minds ever ready to abide and to promote the challenging, onward-moving invitation of Christ: "Up, let us go forward!"

### *"They Were All Filled with the Holy Spirit" (Acts 2:4)*

To Christ's appeal, "Get up, let us be going!" the overly self-confident Peter responds, "Lord, I am ready to go with you to prison and to death" (Luke 22:33). Yet as we all know, Peter's bravado led him down the path of dismal failure. When Charles de Gaulle was the leader of France, French journalists, with tongue in cheek, created a story in which de Gaulle was portrayed as praying a litany at Montmartre in which he included this line: "Sacred Heart of Jesus, trust in me!" While priests and bishops know well the warning against putting too much trust in themselves, I am afraid that far too many in our ranks, and especially those who have succeeded in climbing the ecclesial ladder, have also prayed this comic-tragic and very revealing one-liner.

Are not the powerful and gifted among us especially tempted? There is no other remedy to this illness than to put all our trust in the promptings of the Holy Spirit, in the promise and appeal of Pentecost, which, having ultimately changed Peter and other apostles who had earlier not stood the test of Christ's passion and death, can also change us.

If, in deep faith, we truly contemplate the words: "All were filled with the Holy Spirit," pompous titles like Your Eminence, Your Excellency, and all lesser ecclesial self-serving designations will dissipate like evil ghosts. For in the kingdom of God—the kingdom of right relationships—it is the smallest, nameless, and most humble who are bearers of the comforting and consoling power of the Spirit.

The whole account of the Pentecostal event directs our attention to the prophecy of Joel: "I will pour out my Spirit upon all flesh, / and your sons and your daughters shall prophesy....Even upon my slaves, both men and women, / in those days I will pour out my Spirit; / and they shall prophesy" (Acts 2:17-18). Obviously, there was no mention that servants and handmaids would become priests, since the concept did not yet exist in the young apostolic Church. It was only in the post-apostolic era, as earlier noted, that the term "priest" was cautiously reintroduced in relation to Christ, the true High Priest.

The Pentecost community, marked both by the vision of Christ the Prophet and by the deep conviction of the need for docility and trust in the Holy Spirit, believed both men and women were indisputably earmarked to be humble sharers in Christ's prophetic ministry. Simply put, true Christian women and men are prophetic, liberated, and enspirited persons made so by the power of the Spirit of Christ; and they are endowed with a mission of liberation that always, in our times, calls for vigilance and discernment. Thus, the enduring question for us as Christians and as members of the mystical body of Christ is this: Are we open to the promptings of the Spirit in ourselves and others whatever the cost?

## CHAPTER 4

# THE HISTORICAL BEGINNINGS OF THE PRIESTHOOD

"**D**ay by day, as they spent much time together in the temple, they broke bread at home and ate their food with glad and generous hearts, praising God and having the goodwill of all the people" (Acts 2:46-47). How might we visualize and understand this passage? Perhaps, initially, we might envision a male priest, newly ordained by one of the apostles, celebrating Eucharist for, and with, the gathered, offering the sacrifice of praise. What is certain is that these young apostolic communities, made up of several family groups, knew Jesus' testament quite well: "Do this in memory of me!"

### The Meal Communities of Jerusalem

In coming together, these early meal communities kept their faith-memory alive by sharing their faith, hope, love, and joy. They shared who they were and what they had, but most especially their faith in and praise of God. Very little structure or organization was needed, though we know from the letters of Paul and Acts that great care was taken to provide a sense of order. That is, someone saw to it that things were done in a right way, and that nothing essential was lacking. On second thought, we might more tentatively conclude that someone "presided" at these gatherings, but that all were responsible for the spiritual growth and witness of the community.

The small communities in Africa or the base communities of Latin America might give us some understanding about these original meal communities. However, what should not be overlooked is the important fact that the early faith communities differed noticeably in one respect. In the fledgling Church, people were never deprived of the Eucharist in the absence of an ordained priest. Both Acts and the letters of Paul use the term *oikia,* meaning household-church. Many of these household-churches were identified by women's names. For example, we read of "the household of Stephanas" (1 Corinthians 16:15), and of a couple, "Prisca and Aquila…with their house" (1 Corinthians 16:19). In the Letter to the Romans, Paul greatly praises "Phoebe, a deacon of the church at Cenchreae" (Romans 16:7), and at the end, we find a long list of women and men dedicated to the service of the Gospel and their respective small-faith communities or households.

I am not alone in thinking that women were sometimes responsible for the entire gathering of faith, praise, eucharistic remembrance, and apostolic exhortation in their homes. They did not, and could not, at that time have anticipated our problems, much less understood our scruples concerning the "validity of orders," but they surely were concerned about faithfulness to Christ and, to some degree, about ritual orderliness.

Reflection on these small household gatherings of faith should urge us to return wholeheartedly to, and recapture again, the freshness of the Church's beginnings and should help us to creatively imagine and foster new utopias and workable possibilities for our times.

## *The Multiplicity and Diversity of Charisms*

Both the Acts and the Pauline epistles present us with lively ideas concerning the wealth and diversity of charisms and ministries in primitive Christianity. One thing is most clear. The Tridentine type of priesthood that later developed had no roots in this biblical experience. Nor did the early understanding and expression of celebration point in that direction. The notion of a "one person" team would have been unthinkable: I mean here the idea of one individual being competent to undertake everything for all people. In fact, the "one person" team is, in itself, antievangelical. While today's good pastors must care for several people and specific groups according to their particular and diverse qualifications, charisms, and levels of readiness, it is the whole community that is responsible for caring about education, celebration, and care of the sick, elderly, and the lonely.

Paul says: "Now you are the body of Christ and individually members of it. And God has appointed in the church first apostles, second prophets, third teachers; then deeds of power, then gifts of healing, forms of assistance, forms of leadership, various kinds of tongues" (1 Corinthians 12:27-30). In this light, we are urged to recognize, discern and, with creative liberty and responsibility, cultivate the growing diversity and differentiation of gifts in every corner of the Church today.

## *Elders (Presbyteroi) of the Early Church and Priests Today*

Etymologically, the modern word "priest" (*prêtre, presbitero, priester*) derives from the Greek word *presbyteroi*, meaning "senior citizens." In the traditional Jewish community, there was an office for senior citizens. Length of life was not so much the decisive factor as were wisdom and availability. In Jewish tradition, a group of elders existed side by side with the various priestly and Levitical classes.

There was never any thought of isolating an elder from the group which was always and substantially a collegial institution. Together, the elders offered advice and guidance to the community in cooperation with the priests.

Also, it is an indisputable fact that, within the early Christian community, deeply influenced by its Jewish tradition, no one, single elder ever governed unilaterally. Essentially, it was a cooperative venture of sharing wisdom and authority, marked by a spirit of generosity and availability.

The pastoral letters give us a glimpse of the Church's emerging organizational development circa A.D. 100. A relatively small group of elders (*presbyteroi*) exercised a type of collegial presidency within the assembly for the good of the community. Some were also entrusted by the community with the ministries of preaching and teaching. While these were considered honored services, those engaged in them were never perceived as superior, nor as having been given any particular title or distinction that would elevate or separate them from the assembly. "Let the elders who rule well be considered worthy of double honor, especially those who labor in preaching and teaching" (1 Timothy 5:17).

Thus, it would have been unthinkable to create and foster Christian communities without an established college of elders, as Paul's instructions to Titus point out: "I left you behind in Crete for this reason, so that you should put in order what remained to be done and should appoint elders in every town..." (Titus 1:5).

At this stage in the Church's development, the pastoral letters also introduce the selection of bishops. Although concrete rules or criteria for the choosing of bishops and deacons were already in place, they were always understood and enacted within a larger collegial framework. Moreover, for the sake of peace and giving witness, order was also stressed.

Deep concern and loving care for the sick were at the heart of these small Christian communities, so clearly revealed in the Letter of James: "Are any among you sick? They should call for the elders of the church and have them pray over them, anointing them with oil in the name of the Lord" (James 5:14). Generally, this text is understood in the context of a collegial setting whereby the rite of anointing was celebrated by the elders. It was truly a liturgical experience without the trappings of ritualism.

All over the world today, people are overwhelmingly and persistently recommending that Church authorities entrust the sacrament of the sick to qualified nurses, doctors, lay pastoral associates, or groups of senior citizens who, in a collegial way, can and do visit and care for the sick and elderly. Retired women and men are a largely untapped reservoir for various church ministries. Many of these people have not only theological, pastoral, and clinical training, but also have a profound spirituality equal to, or greater than, some priests and bishops. What nonsense it is to lament the lack of priestly vocations when divine Providence offers us such a plethora of willing and able adults right before our very eyes! These gifted emissaries of God provide us not only with timely opportunities to replenish the Church and liberate her from old rigidities and ritualism, but also to promote collegiality on all levels.

## CHAPTER 5

# THE HISTORICAL DEVELOPMENT OF THE PRIESTLY IMAGE

When I chose to become a priest, the priestly image was considerably less stereotypical (especially in religious orders and congregations) than was the case in previous centuries. At that time, as is the case today, there were also several priestly and lay religious orders with diverse and distinguishing spiritualities blessed with an abundance of gifts for a plurality of ministries.

In the secular priesthood, however, the overwhelming image of the "omnipotent" pastor continued to assert itself. Typically, the one-dimensional Tridentine parish priest was characterized by uniformity, unquestioning obedience, and a general lack of creativity. Pastors, pastoral assistants, and chaplains submissive to their bishops were, however, "compensated" by a priestly regime that promoted control over the faithful. A glimpse of the past may help us to see how this came about and also help us to make reasonable projections for the future—one that we can well say has already begun.

## Bishops and Priests as Martyrs

The word "martyr" originally meant witness to the faith. In that sense, the apostles, their successors, and indeed all believers in every age were and are called to render witness to Jesus Christ, his Gospel, and the salvific plan of God. The earliest bishops normally did not have any more Christians in their dioceses than a pastor might have in a given parish nowadays. The relatively small size of the dioceses enabled bishops to be close to the people. They neither owned palatial homes nor lived a life of opulence and privilege. In every external way, they lived on the same level as their Christian brothers and sisters. What truly distinguished them from most of the faithful was their tangible witness to the death and Resurrection of Jesus as willing candidates for martyrdom. In fact, this was constitutive to their consecration.

By the middle of the second century, bishops or overseers were leaders alongside the elders in their respective dioceses. It was not yet clearly settled as to how they differed overall from the elders. One thing was certain, however. None had aristocratic yearnings or tendencies. From time to time throughout the history of the Church, many became convincing role models of the priest as martyr-witness. In most recent decades, this image is especially evident in Latin America where many, if not all, bishops and priests alike stand on the side of the poor, risking martyrdom at the hands of the wealthy. It is this exemplary quality that distinguishes them from other bishops and prelates tied to pompous ambition, aristocratic attitudes, overblown titles, and self-serving authoritarian behavior.

## Princes of the Church in the Constantinian Era

With the victory of Constantine and the subsequent alliance the Church made with the emperor and the highborn, a new and shocking paradigm of a monarchical Church materialized—a paradigm which was made visible most especially by those bishops who gladly accepted the spoils of privilege and class. Freed of poverty, persecution, and martyrdom, tragically they lost, in large part, the freedom for which Christ had liberated us all.

Constantine and subsequent emperors, kings, and princes shrewdly understood that a Church whose leaders were privileged by civil decree and therefore dependent on the throne could prove to be quite useful to their falsely "sacralized" power. The anointing of kings by the bishop of the empire or the kingdom was an horrific symbol of "priests of the kings" of a "glorious" Church. Given that "logic," it should not be surprising that, at the height of this unholy alliance among emperors, Church officials, and even popes, the question as to who was the mightiest should arise over time. And all this in the name of God in Christ Jesus! While it may have been perceived by ecclesial leaders as the rising glory of the Church, it was, to the contrary, the Church's total downfall, if understood in the light of Jesus' calling as the "Son of Man," in his baptismal consecration in the Jordan, and finally in the shedding of his blood.

Wherever the insidious impulse exists in any religion to share power with civil authorities in such a manner as this, engraved on its very walls are the satanic temptations totally unmasked by Christ the prophet as revealed in the temptation midrash in Matthew's Gospel.

Three glaring examples are sufficient to highlight the operative Constantinian monarchical paradigm of priesthood in contrast to the baptismal paradigm of the nonviolent Servant of God.

*The career system.* One of my former students, a marvelous priest, sought my advice about whether he should accept an offer to enter the diplomatic service of the Church. At first, I was reluctant to express an opinion, but finally I said that the present form of the diplomatic corps was not attractive in the light of the Gospel, but a smart and humble priest could do a lot of good and prevent enormous evil. Therefore, why not use this opportunity to render the best possible service within the system, which of its true nature is not evil? As I spoke, I had in mind great men like John XXIII, who in the diplomatic corps, really served the kingdom of God and the well-being of many people.

Only much later did I have occasion to read what Giuseppe Roncalli wrote in a letter dated November 24, 1928: "Gladly did I leave Rome. It annoyed me to be faced with all this meanness. Everyone is eager to get his appointment, to have a career, and is constantly busy with the gossip about promotion. What a degradation of the priestly life!"

Sometime later, my priest friend returned to tell me that he had given up his career after having gotten one promotion after another and finally hearing: "One day you will even be a cardinal!" He said, "The shock came one night in a dream when I saw myself as a cardinal." Personally, I must admit that I was simultaneously sorry and glad—sorry that the diplomatic service lost this wonderful man, but glad that he had resisted the temptations of the office.

Presently, there are approximately seventeen pompous titles and promotions offered by the Vatican. In an earlier time, Saint Philip Neri, a great priest and humorist, tried to deter priests from succumbing to these ridiculous lures with humor, and not without a little sarcasm at times. Perhaps it is time to recover our best humor and use it to nonviolently protest the antievangelical career system still very much alive today.

*Pomp and Circumstance.* When I came to Rome as a young lecturer, I assisted in a major solemn ceremony in the Church of Saint Peter. The pope was carried on a throne, accompanied by Italian men of high rank dressed in all their noble garb. Following the pope were cardinals swathed in purple robes with the trappings of a thirty-foot train gingerly carried by seminarians. What a comedy of errors! Indeed, what a parody! When some years later Pius XII cut the cauda (train) to ten feet, mighty cardinals balked furiously. Thankfully, things have improved since that time.

*Property and Power Politics.* In 1870, when Pius IX lost the Papal States, and with them, his political power, he and his successors made themselves prisoners of the Vatican, vowing never to leave until these large holdings were restored. In 1929, nearly sixty years later, Pius XI had the courage to relinquish this useless fight that had, all too long, supported a lost and outdated system. Not surprisingly, it was only in 1958 that a pope named John XXIII wandered beyond the Vatican principality to make pastoral visits to the people.

These and other similar occurrences have nothing to do with a hostile or criminal history. Yet, recalling these experiences serves the Church, especially the priesthood, insofar as we learn from these experiences and have the courage to rid the Church and priesthood of all the implications of the Constantinian paradigm once and for all.

All this aside, it must be pointed out that there were always movements within the Church urging a recovery and restoration of priestly origins rooted in the rallying cry of Jesus: "Up, let us go forward!" Allow two exemplary bishops of Milan to speak to this. In the fourth century, with courage and great personal risk, Saint Ambrose compelled the emperor to do penance for the bloodshed he caused before he could be readmitted to the Church. Saint Charles Borromeo, made cardinal as a young man by his uncle-pope, reduced the number of his servants to a "mere" dozen, nearly causing an upheaval. Toward the end of his life, however, Charles not only did away with all his servants, he also bore upon his shoulders his very own bed, on which lay a poor man, a real and symbolic gesture that revealed his contrition for such an earlier ignoble priestly lifestyle.

Time and again, the power of the Holy Spirit and the splendor of the Gospel renew the face of the earth and the Church. Clearly, the power of the Spirit was revealed in this century when all of Christendom believed that, through the wisdom and guidance of Pope John XXIII, the truth and originality of the Gospel triumphed over faulty human traditions.

## The Nonviolent Revolution of the Monastic Movement

Once peace was established between the Roman Empire and the Church, the masses streamed into the Church. It was dubious, however, how many were truly converted. Becoming a Christian was no longer a choice to suffer and risk one's life in the name of Christ. Instead, it proved to be a profitable venture for many, especially for bishops and priests.

Three centuries of martyrdom, however, were not in vain, since, from the inception of Constantinian rule, countless numbers of Christians came to realize that the unholy alliance between "throne and altar" was dangerous and ruinous to the purity of the faith. Even in Constantinople where Constantine's successors reigned, there were clairvoyant and unwavering bishops such as Gregory of Nazianzus and John Chrysostom who courageously lived the paradigm of the nonviolent, humble, suffering Servant of God by unmasking the falsely sacralized powers of pomp and privilege. These men remained faithful to the early monastic movement as well and, because of their steadfastness, they suffered greatly.

The rise of the monastic movement in the fourth century was a prophetic, nonviolent protest against the Constantinian model of Church and priesthood. It was a movement on the scale of a revolution. While monks from East to West did not, in any way, promote an exodus from the Church, they did champion—in an original, clear, and uncompromising way—the restoration of the Church's calling to faithfully follow and embody Jesus, the nonviolent Servant of God. Nor did they experience a dearth of religious vocations as is the case today. Insofar as fervent Christians saw them as Christian communities deeply in love with Jesus and his Church, as was the case of the meal communities of the first century, people flocked to them.

Originally, monks were mostly laymen, but there were also some priests. At the very least, abbots were ordained. It soon became evident that the best monasteries were excellent schools for future bishops. Choosing bishops from monasteries (especially in the eastern part of the empire) was an antidote to the evil effects of the alliance between throne and altar.

The history of monasticism is a fascinating study that reveals the ambiguities of great enthusiasm and great sadness in the Church. The Constantinian Church often invaded and looted monasteries of their treasures in order to gift the ecclesial elite and, yes, at times, to provide funds for the poor. Still, it must be honestly acknowledged that the raids increasingly became a source of priestly temptation. In every century leading up to the Reformation, a tremendous tension existed between the ongoing reforms of the monastic life and the ever-increasing decay within the Church.

The Church as a whole (including her most courageous reform movements) is always in need of ongoing renewal. Conversion is not a one-time affair. The spiritual doctrine of "ongoing conversion" and the ecclesiological principle of "ongoing reform," *ecclesia semper reformanda,* complete each other. Ever-new departures are necessary and, thanks be to God, they are happening more and more. Personal priestly change and change in the institution of the priesthood are reciprocal endeavors, as it is in the case of religious orders and apostolic communities as well.

## Nonviolent Protest of the Mendicant Orders

When the papacy reached its summit of power and prestige under Innocent III, it was not pure coincidence that the mendicant movement, ushered in by thousands of nonviolent women and men of the pilgrim Church, erupted like a Pentecostal storm. The central and most admirable figure of this movement was Saint Francis of Assisi, the unsurpassed prophet of simplicity and poverty who, in every respect, lived the Gospel of the poor, nonviolent Servant of Yahweh. Nor was it accidental that Francis was as much a prophet of nonviolence as he was a believer in simplicity of life, in truthfulness, and in poverty.

Why did he not aim for the priesthood, he who was deeply spiritual to the core? Gratefully, Francis did accept the diaconate with evangelical hope that the image of priest and bishop would be restored in the light of the Servant of Yahweh, a hope not dissimilar to that of Saint Dominic, the founder of the itinerant order of mendicant preachers (Dominicans).

It would surely be time well spent for all of us, were we to ponder which image of the priesthood animated the great saintly priests of the past, especially the founders of religious orders and congregations of priests. Saint Ignatius of Loyola and Saint Alphonsus Liguori were greatly preoccupied with the search for the true image of the priesthood and brotherhood. The vows that Saint Alphonsus and his first companions took are particularly significant and most tangibly expressive of this quest. They vowed never to strive for any ecclesial honors, titles, or even the episcopacy. Moreover, they were not to accept any honors whatsoever, unless under explicit obedience to do so, and always in relationship to the other vow of giving preference to the most poor and most abandoned.

## Imported and Exported Priests

Spanish and Portuguese conquistadors brought with themselves priests of their nations and cultures. They no doubt intended to "save souls" through baptism, but they did so also with the idea of making submission of newly conquered nations easier.

Before I embarked on my educational and missionary activities in the Philippines, I read and studied a number of books sent to me on this subject. Spanish conquerors brought priests and bishops, sustained by the "crown," with the explicit command to purposefully educate people in the ways of becoming submissive and loyal to the emperor of Spain.

All natives were required to learn Spanish, which became the exclusive tongue of the liturgy. Moreover, indigenous persons could not aspire to the priesthood even if one of their parents was a Spaniard. One reason why indigenous people were not admitted to the priesthood was their asserted inability to live a celibate life. In Latin America, the approach was essentially the same.

Many of these imported priests were far from idealists. What the historian Bartolomé de Las Casas writes about them is quite shocking. Many were as interested in money and riches as they were in "saving souls."

Nonetheless, among those dispatched were several wise and brave priests truly dedicated to the Gospel and to the people they served, and eager, in Pauline fashion, to be all things to all people. Yet their idealism and much of the good they attempted to do were, to a certain extent, thwarted by the overall political and cultural contexts in which they found themselves. In reading the history of the Filipino Church, I was astounded by how many imported and salaried priests had the clear-sightedness and the courage to defend the indigenous people, especially the poor, against the colonialists.

While serving in Africa in the decades after the Second Vatican Council, I learned much about the heroism of missionaries. In visiting so many cemeteries, I discovered that a great number of priests buried there were young men who had died after only serving a few years in that hot climate—young men who were fully aware of personal risk, but who generously volunteered nonetheless. These were men who came with absolutely no intention of supporting the colonial policies of the crown.

Only after the period of decolonization did the Church come to realize how serious and far-reaching were the implications and consequences of having cooperated with the subservient demands of the colonial system.

In almost every part of Africa, the rule of celibacy has had the negative effect of hindering full inculturation in myriad ways. The main reason, of course, was the longtime failure to promote an indigenous clergy. In certain African tribes today, celibacy is quite possible, but in neighboring tribes, it is, at least for the time being, unthinkable. Moreover, the importation of priests from other tribes is an affront to their natural pride.

Only in this century has the Church consecrated Chinese bishops. Previously, the main reasons against it was not celibacy but rather the clinging to a stern European superiority complex. At least, that was the impression given. Happily, this attitude of superiority is disappearing. Once, an Italian missionary in Japan said to me, "Thanks be to God I am here where it is inconceivable to look down upon the Japanese culture as inferior. Quite the opposite is true. There is much we can learn from these people."

Forty years ago, I remember reading in the *Osservatore Romano* this horrendous dictum of a powerful Roman cardinal: "Latin must remain the language of the Church in order to cultivate the barbarians by the Latin superculture." Today, of course, we know that such a view is totally absurd and utterly unthinkable. Still, we must bear the burden of the effects of this past form of alienation.

The startling fact remains that, because of the absolute rule that connected the priesthood in the "Latin Rite" with celibacy, the vast majority of people and communities in Latin America, Africa, and elsewhere were, and still are, generally deprived of the Eucharist. Without a doubt, this is only one of the symptoms of a problematic situation that calls for a new and courageous outlook. The freshness of the religious experience of God and the liberating power of the Gospel must not be blocked or hindered by any form of legalism or idolatry.

## CHAPTER 6

# THE TRIDENTINE MODEL OF PRIESTHOOD AND SEMINARY LIFE

Throughout the Middle Ages, numerous cries rang out against incompetent and pastorally ill-prepared priests and bishops. Despite several brave attempts at reform, the situation did not, in the long run, really change. The liaison between throne and altar favored the nomination or election of bishops and even some popes who had practically no theological, spiritual, and pastoral preparation. Fortunately, reformed orders and monasteries cultivated well-prepared men, but this did not sufficiently offset the problems of the secular clergy. The mass defections of bishops and priests at the time of the Reformation would likely not have happened had the Church at large prepared them well.

### *Undeniable Efforts at Reform*

The Council of Trent earnestly addressed this terrible reality by making better preparation for the priesthood one of its main tasks.

It is fair to say that the Council did the very best it could under the circumstances. As a result of laws that were enacted instituting a Tridentine model of seminary life, the Catholic Church, for several centuries, assured the education of devoted and cultivated clergy. While no blame is intended here, it is important to note that this model was a time-bound education rooted in a timeless traditionalism.

Major seminaries undertook the task of philosophical and theological education, while minor seminaries provided only a remote preparation for the priesthood. However, given the prevailing sociological conditions, recruitment tended to be preferential. While the nobility did not send their first-born, who had to assure the continuity of the family line, younger boys were gladly sent with the understanding that they would become career-minded, high-ranking clerics.

For the poorer classes, it meant a unique opportunity for sons to receive a higher level of education. Minor seminaries also prepared numerous men for other professions such as medicine. It was an education that, in the long run, had a cultural impact on several nations. For example, in some of the African countries that had become independent, it was surprising to see that most of their rising political leaders had completed studies in minor seminaries but, because of the celibacy rule, chose not to become priests.

In the post-Tridentine era, it is an unassailable fact that the educational level of clergy is much higher than that achieved in the Middle Ages. Catholic and mainline Protestant churches were similarly disposed to promoting a well-trained and, more or less, uniform clergy with similar ideals and ideas. But frequently and, I might add, unfortunately, those promoted shared the same ideologies as well.

Trained to know Church law and doctrine accurately, priests unquestioningly conformed to the canonically defined rules of life. Hence, they "knew" once and for all what was required of them. Lacking, however, in this priestly training was any vision of an ongoing formation.

Because of the prevailing system of nominating bishops, most of these candidates emerged from the aristocracy; and the criteria for selection was neither rooted in Scripture nor pastoral concerns. However, it would be a grave injustice were we to judge the post-Tridentine system through the lens of our present understanding and times. In an uncritical way, we might proffer that the Church had done as well as she could given her circumstances at that time. Nor was the Council of Trent responsible for a later time when, under quite different circumstances, the Tridentine reforms became frozen and embalmed.

### The Basic Problem: Separation and Alienation

By the age of nine or ten, young boys were chosen by the local priest according to their intellectual capacities and their character, the latter of which meant, above all, fundamental goodness and an unquestioning obedience. Those who qualified were hermetically sealed in a new environment where they were virtually separated from their family members whom they rarely saw—all this under the guise of "preserving their vocation."

The very worst image, which I still observed in Rome some fifty years ago, was that of the twelve-year-old seminarian required to wear the cassock at all times, even when playing sports. The cassock became the highly sacralized sign of being chosen and set apart.

At that time, a highly esteemed rector of the "Great Seminary" in Rome and preacher of retreats for bishops wrote a book called *Modern Training of Future Priests*. In this book, the author said that, for the sake of the priestly vocation, an "asexual" education was required. Consequently, no women were to be found within seminary walls, not even in the kitchen or the infirmary; nor could young girls or women visit a seminarian. Both parents of a seminarian were not allowed to visit at the same time and in the same parlor. A distressed priest once told me that when he was a seminarian, both his parents had come to tell him that his sister had died. He was allowed to see his father first, whereas his mother was led to a different room on the other side of the seminary.

Similar stories were told to me over the years by ex-seminarians and priests who had come for counseling. I often marveled that they were not more disturbed than they were. Eugen Drewermann could have gathered even more interesting experiences at that time and in that place than what he was able to garner later on in a different situation.

Obviously, this is not the norm for the Tridentine priesthood. Rather, it is one of the most degenerate forms of seminary life, and it is worth mentioning because, even in our times, it has impacted the Vatican and other religious institutions.

One example from the life of Saint Alphonse de Liguori highlights the imitation of past centuries. The family of Alphonse, which belonged to the noble class, destined him as heir to their fortunes and, in that light, provided him with a superior legal education. One of his sisters was engaged to marry a nobleman, whereas two brothers and three sisters were destined for religious life. At the age of five, one sister was entrusted to a monastery of cloistered nuns in order to "prepare her" for her vocation. It is no surprise to learn that later, as a nun, she developed psychological problems.

When Alphonse relinquished his legal post, his pious father would not have been troubled had Alphonse, at that time, desired a clerical career in the higher ecclesial ranks. However, Alphonse who, as a priest, befriended and served the Lazzeroni—the street people of Naples—was perceived by his father as a scandal.

Under the prevailing circumstances, a number of reinforcers and compensations were in place. Younger sons from the nobility were destined from the start to become bishops or, at the very least, canons or monsignors. The average sons of the wealthy and the highly gifted sons of the poor were given an opportunity to reach a higher social status. This is part of the historical background of the evil of careerism, which in some circles still exists today.

Careerism was and is an enormous temptation that separates and alienates candidates and priests from the people. Indeed, it is no pleasure for me to mention this, but we must face this reality, first, in order to understand the particular background of past and present problems and, second, to heal and prevent this kind of social illness from occurring in the future.

Another symptom of the superiority-alienation complex is the use of the expression "perfect chastity," erroneously understood as exclusive to the clerical and religious celibate. To the contrary, according to the explicit doctrine of Vatican II and in evident conformity to the New Testament, all Christians are called to sanctity and perfection. All Christians, thus, are called to perfect chastity as well—but a chastity in accordance with the exigencies of their lifestyle.

Married persons are called to conjugal chastity, which is in no way identical to celibate continence. It is, however, a call to strive for perfect chastity nonetheless. In my opinion, the vocabulary of "perfect chastity" understood as exclusive prerogative of the celibate person is an inauthentic motivation, and invites the risk of alienation.

It is important to address this risk in the light of current criticism. A particular breed of priests bemoans the fact that priestly vocations have considerably diminished since Vatican II. They tend to blame this dearth on the new spirit of freedom and the denial of absolute obedience. What is needed today are not ill-founded and misleading accusations but rather a greater faithfulness to the Gospel and a new flowering of authenticity. All expressions of a superiority complex and all specious motives must be totally unmasked for what they are and completely eradicated in light of the Servant of Yahweh. In the process, the present and undeniable crisis can become a blessed crisis of growth through fruitful endeavors to renounce a shallow priesthood and to promote, in its place, a deeper and more viable priestly life. Without a doubt, we must read the signs of the times, but such a reading is only possible by means of

a renewed faithfulness to the original Christian and priestly vocation embodied in Jesus, the prophet and humble Servant.

## A Timeless Philosophy and Theology

With very few exceptions, seminarians were indoctrinated with
the same timeless philosophy, with the same classical theology, and
with the same unchanging truths, in spite of tremendous cultural
differences. All truths were understood as having fallen directly
from heaven without any consideration given to time-bound and
culture-bound conditions. The conditioning power of the milieu
was never considered, and for the longest time not the slightest
thought was given to the fact that, in faithfulness to the Word incarnate, the Church must always look to ever-new cultural "incar-
nations"—in a word, to inculturation. The only major concern was
the uniformity of the clergy for the purpose of unity. But what kind
of unity? Only recently, given a renewed appreciation for
ecumenism, have we better understood a concept of unity made
possible by reconciled diversity and by a shared concern for ongoing inculturation of the Gospel everywhere and at all times.

In order to sensitively respond to our fundamental question:
What kind of priests does the Church need? we must, of necessity,
raise a number of other salient questions. A very important one is:
What kind of Church is needed for the world of today that can
respond with the deepest level of faithfulness to the Gospel and to
the Lord of history? We must be mindful that the present phase of
human history is marked by a tremendous acceleration of events
and historical change, by a greater knowledge of past history in all
its diversity, by a new understanding of pluralism as mutual enrichment, and, finally, by the need for a more profound discernment.

Another question we might ponder is this: In discerning cultural and global events in the light of the nonviolent Servant of
Yahweh, what are the chances for the people of God working in

tandem with the priesthood to eliminate the age-old slavery of war and the glorification of violence in all its forms?

While we are increasingly more aware of the gradual nature of change, we cannot overlook the fact that some changes are long overdue. We must understand that, in general, the acceleration of historical processes does not permit us the ease of sitting back and remaining passive.

At our present historical juncture, the idea of a completely "uni-formed" clergy with uniform rules determined by one geographical outlook on the globe (namely, a purely Western point of view with centralized powers and complete control) is, at the very worst, an ecclesial monstrosity. At the very best, it would make of the Church an interesting museum. Pope John XXIII understood this well. I never forgot the address he gave to the theologians he had chosen or approved of in preparing the Council. At first, and with visible distaste, he began reading an abstract paper, and then suddenly, he put it aside and said emphatically, "Never forget that the Church is not a museum!"

The spurious idea of reintroducing the Tridentine model of priestly reform as the model and rule for current reform means nothing less than renouncing the present and the future in favor of a past to which we can never return. What is very much at stake here is the very credibility of the priesthood.

During the last century in Germany, a considerable number of clergy received their intellectual formation at state-sponsored universities where the so-called *philosophia perennis* (uniform classical philosophy) was already giving way to a historically conscious world-view that provided greater access to, and a new understanding of, the history of salvation as the heart of theology. In light of this new consciousness and inspiration, great theological geniuses emerged such as Johann Adam Möhler, who shaped dogmatic theology, and Johann Michael Sailer, Johann Baptist Hirscher, and Franz Xavier Linsenmann, who worked out an inspiring, enspirited, and historically dynamic moral theology.

These hope-inspiring attempts at authentic renewal, as well as many other signs of hope in the Church after the French Revolution, were thwarted by the so-called *Restoration*, a reactionary trend in the Church that had its beginnings at the Congress of Vienna in 1816 when the Sacred Alliance between the pope as the absolute head of state of the Church and the absolute emperors of Russia, Prussia, and Austria met for the main purpose of restoring their absolutist powers.

This was indeed an unholy alliance whose worst outcome was the sacralized use of religion, totally contradicting the image of the priest as follower of Jesus Christ, the humble Servant of God, in his program of nonviolence. Furthermore, it was a complete contrast to Jesus' prophetic vision of unmasking the satanic temptations to use religion for the sake of human power (see Matthew 4:8-10). Nor was it without profound negative effects on priestly formation, I might add.

Very shortly after the Second Vatican Council, I was called to the "palace" of the Holy Office. There, Cardinal Pietro Parente, a typical product of Roman Tridentine seminary training and the career-minded priesthood, gave me two warnings: "If you continue in the future as you have done in the past, you will never make a career," and "Now is the time to act as a brake." The reader will readily see how these two points are connected. Indeed, and ever so happily, I will never have a career, nor will I curb my views insofar as they reflect the priestly calling of the nonviolent, humble Servant of Yahweh.

### A Word of Caution: Avoid Generalizations!

Historical and theological inquiry cannot be done without a certain amount of typology. Even so, we must be most careful not to overgeneralize. Typology tells us that in the Latin Church prior to Vatican II, an astonishing clerical uniformity, stability, obedience, and observance prevailed, sometimes even confounded with unity.

Moreover, a good number of priests were most faithful to regular prayer and deeply zealous in their quest to "save souls."

At this point, however, generalization must cease. It must be pointed out that, in every century and no less so in the past two centuries, there were always extraordinary priests imbued with originality and creativity who escaped the norm. It seems to me that one great priestly personality can more deeply influence the world for good than can a hundred mediocre carbon copies of the robotic and routinized priesthood.

Among the great were Saint Ignatius of Loyola, Saint Alphonsus de Liguori, and Saint John Neumann. Even Saint Jean-Baptiste Vianney, a genuine representative of the Tridentine clerical model, was a genius in leading people to inner peace and holiness. Proper due must also be given to John Henry Newman, the convert and ecclesial giant among Catholic priests of the nineteenth century who received his early formation in the Oxford movement and who, in his old age, was named a cardinal. Any effort to describe his contributions to the renewal of priestly formation would indeed fill a tome.

Bartholomew Holzhauser (1613-1658), a secular priest, was also an outstanding example of what one charismatic personality can do to contribute to the renewal of the Church. Throughout the Thirty Years' War, he succeeded in persuading many parish priests to live a common life, sharing all things, especially prayer and pastoral ministry. These priests were models of a "house of prayer." All over Bavaria and Austria, there arose centers for genuine Church reform that witnessed to the reality that the Holy Breath (*ruah*) blows where she wills.

### Mature Priestly Vocations

Interesting is the fact that most of those exemplary men entered the priesthood at a mature age with already enriched life experiences. All of the canonized Redemptorist priests also entered the priesthood much later in life, such as Saints Alphonsus, Clement Hofbauer, and John Nepomucene Neumann, the apostle of immigrants in the United States who, with incredible energy and foresight, organized a system of Catholic schools. Peter Donders, the humble servant of lepers, and a strong prophetic voice against the institution of slavery, was a major forerunner of the worker-priest movement. The great converts and other "late vocations," which is to say mature people, well-formed intellectually and socially, who responded to the call were a kind of bridge between clerics exposed to the dangers of separation and alienation and the real life, culture, and milieu in which people lived.

### Saint Alphonse de Liguori, Exemplar of "One of Us"

Around seventeen years of age, Alphonse de Liguori completed, with high honors, the doctorate of civil jurisprudence and canon law. Considered at twenty-seven to be one of the most admired lawyers in Naples, he turned, as he expressed it, "away from the world."

What kind of world did he mean when he said, "World, now I know you!"? It was a world in which a profitable and ostentatious religion offered prestigious posts and pompous titles to likely candidates. He turned his back on a world that typified a kind of "pious polytheism," a mix of prestige, profit, and pomp, with God stirred into the bargain. This mixture raises for our consideration the question: "What kind of God?"

For many priests, the Tridentine God was imaged as one who sided with the mighty and the ecclesial caste. Polytheism of this kind could survive well, even in promoting the articles of the Catholic faith, as long as the superiority complex of the priestly elite was not unmasked or overcome.

Immediately after his ordination, Alphonse continued to radically oppose this regal and elitist image of God by totally and creatively immersing himself in ministry to the poor, most especially to the outcast and the despised. This immersion was, in fact, the fundamental reason for his exodus from that "world" of the rich, privileged, and mighty but, above all, the "world" understood in the worse sense—the sacralized abuse of religion in favor of power and prestige.

As already noted, Alphonse's primary dedication was to the Lazzeroni. Not only did he care for the homeless but, even more, he made them coworkers in building up confraternities among their own class. He organized "evening schools of prayer" in which these people were actively and creatively involved. His genius was not so much revealed in his loving care for the poor as it was in his respect for them, exemplified in his willingness to honor them through a generous advance of trust, even if his efforts did not immediately bear fruit.

His father, a self-conscious nobleman, was simultaneously outraged and ashamed. For years he did not speak to his son who, in his eyes, betrayed the dignity of the family. One day the old nobleman was passing by a church overflowing with people, and a lovely song lured him. Upon entering, the old aristocrat was surprised to see his son whom he had despised singing the Good News from the pulpit and enchanting the faithful with his radiance. That experience was a moment of conversion for the old man, who wished not only to enter this newly founded congregation but also to become a lay brother. The realistic Alphonse, on the other hand, did not accept him.

The first companions of Alphonse, those who cared for the deprived and outcasts of Naples, and who later provided pastoral care for the rural poor, were all men who became priests later in life. It was in the spirit of a loving, nonviolent protest against some of the greater evils in the Church at that time that, apart from the three traditional vows, they added two totally new vows: to give preferential respect and care to the poor, despised, and neglected; and never to seek or accept ecclesial honors, privileges, titles, or even a bishopric in the Church.

In the years in which Alphonse studied theology, among his professors, especially those who taught moral theology, a strong penchant for rigorism prevailed. It was difficult for Alphonse to rid himself of this tendency. What enabled him to do this? In my eyes, it was his threefold exodus I would describe thusly: his departure *from* the world of privilege *to* his radical turning to the poor and despised; his departure *from* cultural pride *to* his turning to the simple ones from whom he learned simplicity; and, lastly, his departure *from* that pious world that abused religion for personal and collective gain *to* the heart and vision of Christ, the Suffering Servant of Yahweh. Again, I would like to refer to Matthew 4:1-11 in which Jesus is described as one who unmasks the satanic temptations to use religion for earthly profit, self-exaltation, and power over others.

## Strange Disputes over the Validity of Ordination

The ridiculous argument as to who, among Jesus' chosen followers, would be distinguished by rank did not end with these early disciples. In fact, the age-old question was revisited time and again in more sordid ways in Constantinian Christendom than ever could have been imagined by those simple fishermen. Innumerable arguments and questions surrounding the ritual validity of the sacraments, and most especially that of ordination, loomed large in that era as they continue to do to this day.

Two years ago when I was in Prague, I had the uplifting experience of being a guest of a gathering of several Catholic groups who, during a long period of persecution, had lived underground and had clandestinely ordained a number of priests, some of whom were married men. What a spirit of faith, dedication, and simplicity! Without question, these men and their families are absolutely wonderful Christians.

One problem that needlessly vexed these priests was doubt about the validity of ordination—a doubt fostered by some Church authorities. These priests and bishops were ordained in a carefully protected and clandestine manner after Pope Pius XII had personally given permission, though he avoided normal diplomatic channels as a cautionary measure in view of Communist secret service operations at that time. I was fortunate to have met quite a number of these priests and some of the bishops, among whom was one who was consecrated in great secrecy by the former bishop of Augsburg.

This particular bishop was one of the bravest and most influential pioneers of these underground ordinations. He was, without a doubt, a bright and gifted person distinguished by courage and foresight. Unfortunately, some narrow-minded Roman bureaucrats claimed that this bishop was psychologically unbalanced and, therefore, his ordination may have been invalid.

My reaction to that egregious statement? If an asserted, but not a proved, psychological imbalance is reason to doubt the validity of his ordination, then we may never overcome doubts about whole generations of priests, for there were surely thousands of bishops throughout history (including bishops in our own times) who were more unbalanced than this bishop who, unfortunately, cannot defend himself since he is dead.

To require priests who were ordained in the underground, especially married ones, to be "reordained" conditionally is totally ingenuous and deprecating. People refer to this as "superordination" and find it distasteful and degrading. Some grudgingly accept this mandate, while others simply cannot. Has the Church not enough real problems to solve without creating artificial ones? I truly believe that these priests are genuine, living reminders of Jesus, Son of Man, "one of us," in an outstanding way. Should they not be acknowledged as a prototype of the priesthood of tomorrow? I certainly think so.

When I was a young moral theologian, several scrupulous priests, including some in high positions, who anguished over the validity of ordination came to me for counseling. Would you believe that their most vexing questions were whether or not they had touched at once the chalice, paten, and altar bread at ordination (at that time, this was considered a substantial sign of validity); and if they did not, should then all subsequent celebrations of the Mass and sacraments be considered invalid? Thankfully, Pope Pius XII brought all this nonsense to an end by officially declaring that this ritual had absolutely nothing to do with validity.

Today, in view of ecumenism, the arguments surrounding the validity of orders are particularly appalling. Anglican priest converts must still be ordained conditionally, and the major dispute against validity is rather strange indeed. It is argued that Anglican bishops who earlier had broken away from the Catholic Church during the Reformation did not really know what the sacrament of priesthood and ordination meant and, therefore, they might not have had the right intention.

If this argument proves to be weighty in Roman eyes, then we had better start "reordaining" all our own priests and bishops as well. But who should do this? We might ask ourselves whether or not the Renaissance bishops of the Catholic Church themselves had the right intention. Did they better know what priesthood meant? Did the immoral seventeen-year-old elected Pope John XII know any better what it meant, before God, to be a bishop, not to mention what it meant to be the Bishop of Rome? The greater part of wisdom would be to give up these hollow arguments and concerns and search instead for a more profound understanding and meaning of apostolic succession in line with the *entire* Gospel of Jesus Christ.

If this kind of ritualism prevails, there will be particularly serious problems surrounding the question of uninterrupted succession of the bishops of Rome. History reminds us anew that quite a number of popes were simonists who were elected in less than an authentic manner. Often no one knew who really was the successor of Peter, particularly in those decades when there were two or three popes, some of whom were truly unworthy men. Doubtless, there is an apostolic line in the Church that, if understood in a much more profound sense, can more easily help us end these zany arguments, especially as we endeavor to promote ecumenism.

## For the Sake of Humor

Surely, our own sense of humor is, in some way, a small reflection of the great humor of God. Were it otherwise, how could God put up with us ever so patiently? Humor is indeed a liberating and healing virtue.

As to the question of validity, from a biological perspective, some men have more female than male elements in their genetic code (DNA); externally, however, they appear to be male. If, according to Vatican teaching, women cannot validly be ordained, how then do we explain the ordination of priests and bishops with genetic codes that reveal them to be more like women? As regards the biologically based argument used by the Vatican to discriminate against women's ordination, here is a second but no less humorous question. How do we judge the validity of the ordination of men who, according to their DNA, are men but exhibit an effeminate behavior?

The moral of the story is this: when we begin with wrong premises, reasonable and sensible solutions can never be achieved. Illusory, ill-founded, and contrived arguments might best be overcome, at least in part, by a good sense of humor.

## What Kind of Moral Theology for the Church?

Our excursion through the strange world of ritualism brings us back to a central question about the priest of the future. Given that priests were, in part, malformed by the negative effects of moralism and ritualism stemming from a Tridentine model, it raises a basic question as to what kind of moral theology should the ideal priest of today and tomorrow be taught, not only for the sake of his own self-understanding, but also for the sake of his ministry of proclaiming the Good News of which moral teaching is an essential part?

Most ritualistic-oriented, anguished, and troubled priests of past centuries were more or less casualties of the late Roman type of moral theology. They were required to learn a long list of mortal sins with accurate classifications, a number of which were considered exceptionless (*ex toto genere*). Hundreds of questions about mortal sins were treated in relation to ritual precepts and, all too frequently, within the dark cloud of taboos.

The teaching of a narrow concept of obedience and loyalty led to a repressive attitude in which all critical questions touching on Church authority were crushed. A mediocre and less intelligent spirit could survive in a climate that tended to obliterate serious doubts about the system itself. Of course, more intelligent seminarians and priests had greater trouble in repressing their doubts about the legitimacy of such a system of morals and, therefore, in one way or another, suffered psychologically.

Somehow, many did find a way out. There were hundreds of minor questions open for discussion, and since disputes of that kind could go on endlessly, some had the feeling that, at the very least, there was some development of the virtue of discernment. But these "open questions" were, for the most part, not the vital concerns of ordinary people.

Still another serious problem centered around the then commonly used manuals of Roman moral theology that offered a very constricted view of grace, which was understood as divine assistance in fulfilling all laws and prescriptions faithfully. What a long way that was from Saint Paul's vision of the law of grace: "You are not under law, but under grace" (Romans 6:14). Add to this entire problem the enormous number of ecclesial penal laws, to say nothing of a most elaborate system of honors and titles that were available to the submissive priest. What a degradation of priestly life it is when a rightful holy fear of God is replaced or mixed with such a system of penalties and promises!

B. F. Skinner, the unsurpassed master of manipulation of rats and apes, has asserted that human beings can be almost as well manipulated as rats and apes by a similar, elaborate mixture of pleasurable rewards and frightening threats. I think that this is true only for mediocre and weak people, especially if they are caught in a system of legalistic moralism combined with a congenial pedagogy that promotes a one-sided emphasis on rewards and threats. Unfortunately, Skinner was unable to know a moral theology and pedagogy based on the experience of gratuity and generosity. It would be a shame if Church leaders today were unaware of, or insensitive to, the liberating power of a life no longer under law, but under grace.

If priests are shaped by the Roman type of casuistic and legalistic morals and, at the same time, are exposed to the lure of ecclesiastical honors, they would, indeed, require an extraordinary level of purity of intention and a very strong and grateful faith to overcome the temptations that arise from within and without—especially if the impact of their earlier formation is reinforced by an ecclesiastical environment impregnated by the satanic temptations to "use" religion and religious positions for self-exaltation and as satisfaction of a lust for power.

After all, it is no wonder, in certain parts of the world where a moralistic tradition and an elaborate system of promotion and penalties are still especially strong, that priests are generally perceived, in one sense, as cheaters and, in milder terms, as "squinters." They are perceived as always looking first and foremost to the system of penalties and rewards, with the oft-asked question ever on their minds: how would this behavior affect my personal honor and career? Sadly, it is often only after this self-serving consideration is satisfied that the question about truth is raised. Fortunately, many mature priests who had to endure a manualistic and legalistic formation were not deeply affected, since they were able to look, above all, to the Gospel and the example of Jesus and the saints.

Since the role of the priest is primarily that of a credible witness, it is of the utmost importance that all Church structures, all basic relationships within the Church, and the whole of moral formation promote and encourage absolute sincerity and transparency. This endeavor also coincides with the critical need to prevent the development of all ecclesiogenic pathologies. Anything that could damage the absolute requirement for priestly sincerity and reliability can never be offered as an acceptable sacrifice to God.

## Overextending the Role of Priests

Frequently, the Tridentine priest, especially in the nineteenth century, was overburdened by the number of roles he was required to take on and, because of that, he suffered greatly. The priest had to be a good pastor, a fervent confessor, an admirable preacher, a teacher of the law, and, frequently, a controller, especially in presiding over the sacrament of penance. Moreover, he had to teach catechetics, administer parish properties and finances, and God only knows what else.

Essentially, the historical roles of the papacy served as a prototype for the local priest. The pope was and still is the bishop of Rome, the primate of Italy, and the patriarch of the West and of most continents. Over time, popes gradually reserved for themselves the appointment of ever more bishops. In his book *De Consideratione,* which contains the sermons from a retreat preached for Pope Eugene III, Saint Bernard sharply warns in no uncertain terms against all these kinds of overextended activities of the papacy:

> All day I hear in your palace the noise of laws and laws. And what kind of laws but those of the Emperor Justinian! Nothing do I hear of the law in which my heart rejoices—the law of love. You waste most of your time on matters of politics. There you are surrounded by flatterers, liars, and adulterers looking for favors. Save your precious time for meditating on the gospel and preach it joyously....

In our times, the pope is committed to appointing almost all of the four thousand or so bishops of the world and to maintaining an enormous apparatus for controlling appointments of theologians and their teachings around the globe, leaving little room for subsidiarity. He intends to be the worldwide overseer also and, most recently, the very embodiment of the moral teacher. Like an absolute monarch, it is totally left to him to widen or limit the degree of collegial and synodal cooperation. Is this not more than a glaring symbol of the overextended clergy? Does papal management and control of this magnitude truly favor genuine priestly vocations and a biblically grounded understanding of priesthood and of bishops?

In parallel fashion, might we not ask if overextended priests and bishops still have time for ongoing formation and updating in theology, spirituality, and the human sciences? Do they have sufficient time for prayer, for learning anew the art of prayer, and the integration of life and prayer?

## CHAPTER 7

# QUESTIONS SURROUNDING THE ISSUE OF CELIBACY

In speaking about celibacy for the sake of the kingdom of God, we must most carefully distinguish between celibacy as freely chosen in itself and celibacy freely chosen as an absolute condition for priestly ordination.

### Critical Considerations

Further considerations lead us to distinguish between genuinely free assent to celibacy as the expected norm for the religious priesthood and, on the other hand, free assent not so much for its intrinsic value and attraction, but because it is the absolute condition for becoming a priest. Consenting because law requires it can, in the course of time, become a source of joy with an ever-deepening understanding of its meaning and beauty, or it can increasingly become a heavy burden.

Each priest lives his celibacy uniquely in his particular cultural and social context. We shall come to see that the social context in most countries today differs greatly from that which existed at the time when the law, which connected priesthood with celibacy, came into existence in the Latin Church.

### Good Luck

Comparing authentic married love and faithfulness to an authentic celibate life will be my starting point for this discussion, for I believe that a happy marriage is a worthy image for a genuine and charismatically lived celibacy.

A friend of mine invited me to celebrate, with his radiant wife, Dorothee, their twenty-fifth wedding anniversary. Since I could not attend, Eric later told me of a conversation he had with his wife at the celebration. In the presence of all their friends and guests, he said to his wife, "What good luck! We love each other today just as we did on the first day of our marriage." Upon hearing those words, Dorothee's facial expression changed and, in that moment, realizing that he had blundered, Eric responded essentially in these words:

> I am guilty for understating our life together. Without a doubt, of necessity, our love had to deepen and become stronger. In the process, we have learned to accept our mutual shadows which made the light more brilliant. Over the years, we have helped each other deal reasonably well with our weaknesses. When we entered into this alliance we were sufficiently mature, but the learning process was not always very romantic. Often we had to ask for forgiveness. And, oh, how very much our mutual love grew in the sharing of it with our four children, most especially in the learning process that was so necessary in rearing our suffering epileptic son, Gerald! Thank you so much, Dorothee. You have always and most generously trusted me from the outset, and in the process we both came to discover more and more our own interior resources. Let us hope that, in the years to come, our love will continue to grow, blossom, and ripen!

In view of these wise and salient thoughts, I have often reflected on my own way of living and loving my celibacy in and through the ever-growing love of Christ who, in my experience, has expressed his love for me with infinite generosity and patience. Without question, it was through love that God had chosen me for the priestly life, and I can truthfully say that it was through love that I responded. Even more than Eric and Dorothee, I had to learn what this kind of love demanded and implied. It was a long learning process, and I fully realize that it must continue. My fond hope is that I shall always be a good learner, open to new thought and possibilities. Thanks be to God, there were no grave crises along my way, but there were many faults and omissions. To allow the fire of the Spirit to cleanse my motives and, at the same time, awaken in me a deeper spirit of humility and generosity was not always "romantic."

It was only gradually that I came to learn that the Saving Christ meets and tests me most especially through troubled people such as the divorced who, surrounded by difficulty, suffer all the more from judgmental attitudes, even from the Church. Although I am an old man, I am very much aware that I am little more than a learner.

To live celibacy and to love celibately in today's world is a venture that can be reasonably undertaken only when we place our trust, not in ourselves, but in God alone, and remain open to the guidance of Holy Mystery at all times.

Thank you, Eric and Dorothee, for presenting me with such a wonderful lesson! May it become fruitful in my life and in the life of my many priestly celibate peers!

## In Spite of Difficulties

Once I preached a mission for refugees in which, in the first few days, only one adult male participated. For whatever reasons, the other men in the town promised each other they would not come. Wondering why, I approached the only couple who came and participated faithfully and enthusiastically. In the course of our discussion, the gracious wife told me her personal story. In her youth, she had given some thought to becoming a religious, but subsequently she fell in love with Robert. Caught in a dilemma, she approached her confessor and asked, "What might better please God—becoming a nun or encouraging a man to embrace the faith?" She was absolutely sure that it would not be difficult to win Robert over, as he was a truly marvelous man. As it turned out, she fully succeeded in her quest.

It was through the efforts of her very capable and fervent husband that we were able to win over almost all of the Catholic men of that small town. His wonderful wife had originally taken a great risk and won a hundredfold. So can it also be for many young men who feel that promising lifelong celibacy is a risk. If priests are truly in love with God and his people, including the most troubled and difficult ones, why should they not take the risk and, knowing well their human limitations, ask for a dispensation in the event that celibacy cannot be lived?

Some young people may be enthusiastic for God and passionate about bringing people closer to God, but not at all excited about celibacy, especially if they fear the wrath of others and the possibility of harsh treatment should they not succeed in living celibacy faithfully. These young people must have the courage to take the risk alone. No one can tell others how great the risk will be.

A note of caution is needed, however. There can be some cases in which the confessor or advisor may have to point out that the risk could be too disproportionate. On the other hand, the decision to take the risk might be made much easier and be less anguishing were Church authorities more sensitive and comprehensive in their outlook and understanding when, in spite of all best efforts, fervent priests of any age come to realize they cannot always perfectly live a celibate life.

From having taught and preached retreats to thousands of priests around the globe, I came to know a number of them who, after an initial failure, were able to live the celibate priesthood in a humble and fervent way. As is true in marriage, commitment to the celibate life is often stronger, happier, and more authentic after a crisis.

There are many priests who are truly happy, not only in spite of celibacy, but because of it. There are also happy celibate priests who might even be happier and more radiant were they allowed to marry, or had they been ordained as married men. There are priests with deep human and religious qualities who are, nevertheless, troubled by sexual problems such as masturbation—a problem that they were unable to overcome in spite of tremendous efforts; these priests are troubled all the more because of the senselessly over-dramatized way in which the issue of masturbation has been treated in the Church. Often it is not at all a moral but rather a psychic and hormonal problem.

If priests are helped, in a convincing way, to de-dramatize their difficulties, they may, to their own surprise, become gradu-ally and fully liberated. Even if that does not happen, they can still be excellent priests. Some are truly wonderful priests and healers precisely because of problems they face and are attempting to over-come. In fully knowing and accepting their own weaknesses, they often become more humble, understanding, and compassionate toward others in their weaknesses. I suggest that a number of young men would have more readily chosen a celibate priestly life had the problem of masturbation not been unduly dramatized and over-stated.

By contrast, a priest who has successfully lived a celibate life and who has been blessed with the gifts of preaching, teaching, and counseling may very well be tempted, if not by pride, then possibly by vanity. If vanity becomes increasingly tangible, his prob-lem may be even more serious than vanity itself; that is, he could easily become self-satisfied.

A very joyous and sympathetic priest once told me how he was healed of vanity. He pointed out to his parishioners that hon-est criticism is a virtue, and that at times they are entitled—in fact, obliged—to criticize their pastor, as it could very well turn out to be an act of charity. One parishioner, taking his words to heart, told this good pastor on the following Sunday, "My Lordship, during your sermon, I just could not get over my impression of hearing the cock of Peter singing his own praise with his beautiful voice." My old friend told me that that remark had hurt him very much, but he also said that it greatly helped him in coming down off the dunghill of vanity. In this and other similar cases, I believe what could very well be concluded by many priests is that, in spite of all this, things have gone quite well.

## Celibacy Compared with an Invalid Marriage

It is only in the last few decades that canonists and moralists have discovered and come to terms with the fact that quite a large number of marriages celebrated in the Church might very well be declared invalid since, from the outset, unions of this kind have shown themselves to be so sick and sickening as to have little chance of success, even in spite of goodwill on the part of one or both parties. Although these couples are more or less normal, they are often in character, feeling, and other important respects so radically different as to be strangers to each other, such that their "allergic" reactions to each other simply cannot be overcome or healed. Fully realizing that differences are often a source of mutual enrichment, we must concede there are, nonetheless, some differences that are so great that living together for a lifetime could simply make the couple chronically ill. The Orthodox Churches have long realized that this can happen, and that these marriages can be considered not only dead but even still-born from the very beginning.

Similarly, this can happen and frequently has happened in the celibate life without guilt or, at the very least, without serious guilt. How could a twenty-three-year-old man foresee all the existential problems surrounding the celibate life of a parish priest? This question is even more urgent in view of boys and young men who are completely insulated from life in minor and major seminaries.

We all know quite well a number of fine and well-respected priests whose parishioners were very surprised to hear that they had asked for a dispensation, which nowadays still means laicization (a return to lay life). In some cases, it is not the issue of celibacy but rather a profound experience of hurt I would categorize as "otherliness." I present here one case, but it is hardly an isolated one.

At a common meal on Christmas, an overbearing pastor ranted furiously at a twenty-nine-year-old chaplain because he had followed the example of a well-respected cardinal who, when praying, fully extended his arms. The pastor said to him, "I will get you if you give scandal by not observing the sacred laws of liturgy." Cautiously, the young chaplain replied, "Just as our bishop, the cardinal, observes them?" This simple remark was enough to send the pastor into orbit. With excessive and quite needless anger, the pastor replied, "You must observe the laws of Holy Mother Church and not the example of a cardinal, since you are nothing but a chaplain."

Later that evening, they met again on the stairwell, and the pastor resumed his tirade. Years later, that young man told me that on that evening, he masturbated for the first time, not for pleasure but as an expression of deep frustration. As these explosive bouts continued while he lived there, so, too, did the young associate continue to masturbate as his frustration continued to mount. He sought the aid of a psychotherapist who, in discussion, became convinced that he needed to be freed from his oppressive and wounding environment. He advised him to ask for a dispensation as a necessary prerequisite for having any chance of being healed at all.

Many years later, we met again. In the interim, he married a good woman and reared fine children. Moreover, he became involved in his parish as a religious educator. In fact, his whole family exhibits a fervent missionary spirit, and they are all very happy.

Still, I wonder if his priesthood and celibacy might have been saved under different circumstances, had he not had those repressive and alienating experiences. What might have happened if he had been given the opportunity to live with wholesome priests whose lives could have been mutually enriched through the acceptance of each person's individuality? Perhaps most of us can think of either married or celibate people who have suffered similar traumas because of allergic reactions to personality differences.

The current law, which mandates celibacy as the only door to the ministerial priesthood of the Roman Catholic Church, is poisonous for many because of their experience of an "other Church," rooted in authoritarian structures and marked by negative attitudes, judgment, and legislation from on high. I cannot avoid expressing my opinion regarding the kind of treatment given priests who ask for a dispensation, a treatment that is very similar to, and sometimes harsher than, that applied to the divorced, which, to any degree, is reprehensible.

I had the opportunity of speaking with Pope Paul VI on this very problem; and I discovered he was extremely sensitive to it, such that he even sent troubled priests to me for counseling. Even more, he promised to initiate change. Up until that time, the concordat with the Italian state declared that men who had left the priesthood to marry could not be employed by the state. From the Church's point of view, a married priest with children could be admitted to communion only when he had given proof of total sexual abstinence, living together with his wife as brother and sister. Should he fail even once, the case would again be reserved to Roman authorities. Pope Paul made decisive changes.

Immediately at the beginning of his pontificate, Pope John Paul II adopted a much more rigorous approach than his predecessors. In my eyes, the results are all but encouraging. As a consequence, many former priests marry in a civil ceremony or simply live together with their intended wives without civil approbation. Equally serious is the fact that I have heard several young men say that they no longer have the courage to be ordained to the celibate priesthood because they fear harsh treatment should it happen that they discover later on that they cannot truly live a celibate life.

## Two Different Approaches

For the indissolubility of marriage and celibacy, and for, in fact, the whole of Christian life, there are two very different understandings and practices. One is the path of the Gospel, and that of Saint Paul who sees everything from the perspective of God's graciousness. The other path is the one that unduly emphasizes law, observance, and control by law.

Marriage, as understood from the prevailing perspective of grace, means trusting that God will graciously empower persons to *dare* to commit themselves to the marriage covenant with its promise of lifelong fidelity. Even should troubles and difficulties arise, marriage partners do not give up. Rather, as God continues to give, time and again, an advance of trust, married couples are called to embody this selfsame generosity and trust. God's forgiveness is honored by the asking for, and offering of, forgiveness of faults and failings. Only when it becomes clear that a marriage ceases to be a shared way of salvation and becomes most harmful to personal integrity and health can couples part, all the while still hoping for mutual forgiveness.

While couples ought not enter into the marriage covenant lightly or arbitrarily, success cannot be absolutely guaranteed even in the case of a pondered decision. In spite of goodwill at the outset, there may come a day when such couples discover the union to be so broken as to be irretrievable. Even then, in fact especially then, both parties should trust all the more in God, who graciously offers them a new beginning and urges them to take all things into consideration in order to seek the best possible solution.

From the perspective of law, marriage is based upon a contractual view of sacrament that is indissoluble, made so by the very fact of that law. Even when it is obvious that a broken marriage is totally irreparable, the contractual "sacrament" hangs over a couple's heads like the sword of Damocles. This interpretation of sacrament should be dispensed with once and for all.

Celibacy, as understood from the perspective of law, may lead to the practice of treating a priest who fails as though he were a traitor or a leper, yet ever condemning him to remain a priest under the law—even when it becomes quite evident that the law does not save him. To the contrary, the law not only hurts him; it may even destroy him.

However, if in true Pauline fashion it is rightly understood that all Christians are no longer under a regime of law, but rather under grace, a person who feels called to the celibate priesthood will put all his trust in God's grace, maintain a healthy prayer life, walk wisely, and keep vigilance. Still, we cannot exclude the possibility that it might later become clear that celibacy is not really that person's calling. In that case, one should be lovingly encouraged to ask for a dispensation without fear of being ostracized or despised by the Church.

A cursory look at thousands of years of Buddhist tradition may be of some help in this regard. While Buddhists highly respect the celibate life, they understand that one must never make, save for exceptional cases, an irrevocable commitment. Celibacy, lived for a period of time in one particular Buddhist tradition, is praised as good preparation for a later marriage. While I do not plead for imitation here, I do, however, suggest we undertake a new and more humane look at our tradition, especially in view of rapidly and profoundly changing historical circumstances.

## Celibacy in Its Historical Context

The noted scientist Marcel Légaut one of many who has freely chosen to live a celibate spiritual life, convincingly alerts the Church to the value and benefit of celibacy for the sake of the kingdom of

God. These benefits accrue particularly if full attention is given to the total context in which celibacy is lived. However, he avers, and I agree, that laws that surround special charisms must never be understood as timeless, as though they were a heavenly reality outside the realm of changing history.

## Priestly Celibacy As a Signpost

Priestly celibacy lived faithfully and joyously can be a help and signpost for those who, due to various conditions of life, are forced to live celibately, even though they have not freely chosen to do so. I think of the divorced and the many men and women living a celibate life either because no opportunity for marriage presented itself or because health problems disallowed marrying. Being sympathetic to those who cannot marry could very well be a means of strengthening our desire to more deeply understand our own celibate calling. Even more, it is possible that we may learn from single persons who have come to accept their unchosen life, and who have discovered not only how to make sense of it, but how to live their celibacy fruitfully.

During the protracted war in Russia, an old Russian Orthodox priest who was ill came to me for help. After welcoming him, I asked him the usual question, "How are you and your holy wife?" He replied, "My wife is in heaven, and all my children are dead. Now I am all alone—alone with the Lord and for the Lord." His face was so radiant when he said those words, in utmost simplicity, that I could not help but be deeply moved. For me, it was the best if briefest of all homilies on my own celibate vocation.

If, with God's grace, we priests live an authentic celibate life, this life can be, in the very living of it, a wordless yet powerful message for many single people who have no other alternative. Nevertheless, reflection on this intention and the value of celibacy is not enough. Celibacy should lead us to greater zeal and creativity in doing our utmost for single women and men. At the very least, we should encourage them to live their lives more fruitfully by enabling them to experience the support of the community, especially by creating opportunities to develop meaningful and lasting friendships.

## Celibacy and Population Problems

There is a strong link between celibacy and the issue of population. I will address two aspects relating to the law of priestly celibacy. At the time in which celibate practice and law prevailed, overpopulation was not a problem. Fewer families existed and could not as easily be multiplied as was the case in the industrial urban age. Aristocratic, middle-class, and especially poor families were delighted when their offspring found fulfilling lives as vowed men and women in community or in the secular or religious priesthood. Though overpopulation was not a problem, economic conditions existed that rendered it impossible for some men to marry. Often this was the case in the majority of larger families. As a consequence, a celibate life within large families was considered socially acceptable, and there is little doubt that the celibate priestly life made a positive contribution in the direction of acceptability.

In today's world, overpopulation is unarguably a growing problem. It is, first of all, a matter of preserving the conditions on our planet that allow life to go on. In starker terms, what is ultimately at stake is the planet itself, whose very viability is needed to support all forms of life. Those who freely embrace a celibate life for the sake of the kingdom of right relationships make, at the same time, a relevant contribution to the common good.

Population problems can have an enormous impact on recruiting people for the celibate priesthood and religious life. Given the modern conditions of industrial and postindustrial Western society, the right to marry is considered one of the most basic human rights. However, the present culture, aware of the problems of overpopulation, tends to support, of necessity, a system that encourages one- or two-child families. From this small-family perspective, recruitment to the priesthood is much more problematic than it was in the past.

In view of current population problems, certain past arrangements are worthy of note. It was not uncommon for priests to have widowed mothers and a few female siblings living in the rectory, not merely as housekeepers but especially as friends and companions who, in fact, continued to provide a family life for the priest, some of whom truly embodied an ideal family spirit. Nor should this be understood as siblings having freely renounced marriage for the sake of assisting brother priests. More nearly, it was a question of either choosing a religious vocation or assisting priests when no opportunity for marriage presented itself. Under present conditions, of course, this arrangement is extremely rare.

Over twenty years ago when I taught the clergy of Malta, I discovered that is was, more often than not, a tradition for priests to live with their original families. These men were truly "at home" and ever so happy. As a side effect, priests found it an enormous sacrifice to give up their families in order to serve the Gospel in another country.

Once when I was a guest of a bishop in Italy, I was surprised to see that he had no housekeeper and that he himself had proceeded to prepare our breakfast. When I asked him why this was so, he said that, although he could easily afford to hire help, he chose not to, since it was not feasible for most of his priests. In praising his priests, he also said that many of them were very lonely and spent far too much time watching television.

Another cultural shift linked to celibacy is a philosophical one. Under the ancient and longstanding influence of Stoic and Platonic philosophies, married life was considered somehow degrading, whereas sexual continence was perceived as superior. In an unhealthy way, the Augustinian tradition promoted this view, which later seeped into moral teaching. Today, thankfully, all of Christianity and most other cultures have a much greater and healthier regard for human sexuality, stemming either from religious or various humanistic perspectives.

An especially one-sided philosophy or psychology that emphasizes self-fulfillment is unlikely to find meaning in sexual continence. Of course, celibacy understood in the light of faith is obviously more than sexual continence. Above all, it is joy in the Lord, coupled with generous service to the Gospel on behalf of God's people, which gives sexual continence its deeper meaning, thus making it a positive experience. However, only persons of deep faith can come to this realization.

## Looking for Solutions

There are no simple solutions to complex problems, but some paths can be trod in an effort to overcome them. One path relates to the burning question of friendships among priests in neighboring parishes. I know of some priests who belong to such spiritual groups as the Focolare Movement, which follows the example of Bartholomew Holzhauser. These priests choose to live in small communities of three or four, and are even encouraged by bishops who, in an effort to promote this arrangement, offer them pastorates in neighboring parishes.

A short time ago, I preached a retreat for twenty priests on the occasion of their silver jubilee and found their spirit of friendship admirable. I was delighted to hear that since their ordination, they have yearly spent a week together in prayer and recreation.

## A Community-Building Spirituality

The best response to the danger of loneliness is an inward-looking spirituality based upon the solid teachings of Saints John the Evangelist and Paul—"Christ in us, we in Christ." If rightly understood, this view of spirituality has nothing to do with escapism. The very depth of the experience of Christ-in-me opens up a wonderful horizon for an all-embracing friendship. The Christ-in-me, loving me and being loved by me, enables me to join him, our Savior, in his love for all my brothers and sisters. My love and concern for them is the love of Jesus in and through me. Their loving response in return is part of Christ's own love for me and for them.

Needless to say, this profound mystery is infinitely more than a prescription against loneliness. However, the very real danger of loneliness itself should be sign enough to lead us to discover and probe the depths of a eucharistic spirituality. It is absolutely necessary for presiders at the eucharistic celebration to do so. It is also essential that they continually invite participants to discover meaning for themselves in this community-building spirituality, always prompted, first and foremost, by the Holy Spirit who introduces us all to this blissful mystery. In this way, celibacy is not perceived as a form of segregation from the faithful. To the contrary, celibacy expressed as "life in Christ" and "love in Christ" is the sum and center of the priestly celibate life.

This wonderful intimacy of life in Christ Jesus is the complete antithesis of individualism. Not only are the fetters of individualism destroyed, but every possibility for developing rich relationships, as embodied in the *Abba* prayer at the Last Supper, are renewed. The life of developing intimacy in the *Abba* prayer is a Trinitarian and bridge-building experience within redeemed humanity. It is Jesus, the Redeemer of the world and the Son of God, who, by the power of the Holy Spirit, is praying *Abba* in us, which simultaneously resounds as *Abbuni* (*our* Father), Father of our Lord Jesus Christ, and of us all.

This Trinitarian expression of intimacy opens up all horizons of saving-solidarity, of the community of salvation, of sisterhood and brotherhood, and of all creation. In it, we come to see and honor each other as sons and daughters of the same Father. We also see and honor our call to mutual sharing with, and responsibility for, all created life. The strength of this solidarity is only as great as the depth of our intimacy. Given this understanding, believers entrusted to our pastoral care are never objects of priestly office or ministry. Rather, we are one among all people, receiving from them as much as giving to them. In this understanding, there is no room for the language of "we" and "they." Together, as subjects, we travel the road with, in, and to Jesus Christ, who is the beginning and the end of our journey.

## CHAPTER 8

# THE CONCILIAR AND POST-CONCILIAR IMAGE OF THE PRIEST

During the Second Vatican Council, bishops—and their advisors who were mostly priests—were very much aware that priests expected a clear and meaningful word on their life and ministry in the midst of a changing world and a changing Church. Only at the very end, on December 7, 1965, after a period of serious gestational stress, did the Council Fathers approve such a decree on the ministry and the life of priests.

## Initial Efforts

Earlier in October of 1964, the seventeenth project on the priesthood was proposed to the general assembly and had received heavy criticism. On behalf of West German bishops, Cardinal Julius Dopfner of Munich offered the most serious objection. The text was judged to be thoroughly outside the historical experience of priests and lay people, reflecting as it did a typical unhistorical (timeless) theology and spirituality. The immediate reaction of the great majority of bishops made it perfectly clear that this was the document's most vulnerable point.

In haste, a completely new text was drawn up. Truthfully, the commission made every effort to encompass the joys, hopes, sorrows, and anxieties of today's world which priests had shared with them. However, thirty years after the Council, it must be acknowledged that those who drafted and approved the text were not fully aware of how deep the crisis was, and of the degree of change that would impact on cultures and societies today, as well as those of the future. A realistic prognosis was still lacking, and the Church's sensitivity still needed to grow, even under the duress of much pain and turmoil.

Despite this, it is worthwhile to give considerable attention to this important decree, for in it are found these several significant and relevant points: Priests cannot really serve people unless they are totally familiar with their life conditions, which as a consequence means that priests are meant to live amid the people entrusted to them (paragraph 3). Great emphasis is given to the task of helping people grow toward fuller maturity (paragraph 6). And could we not explicitly say that this point implies the acknowledgment and fostering of the virtue of critique? Another important focus is that priests should give particular preference to the suffering, sick, and poor. Nor should it be overlooked that the decree clearly emphasized the building up of Christian community around the centrality of the Eucharist (paragraph 8).

Even though the Council did not neglect to point out the phenomenon of rapid acceleration of historical processes, how could the Council Fathers not have anticipated the most pressing consequences of this phenomenon—for example, the problems surrounding pluralism and reconciliation—in full acknowledgment of cultural diversity? The decree rightly underlines the importance of a spirit of poverty among priests, but why, then, was it not said that bishops should themselves be moving examples of poverty and simplicity of life? The text also offered rich inspiration for a priestly spirituality as an expression of fraternal solidarity. Last but not least, an explicit appeal was made to priests to conscientiously assess themselves in the light of those adaptations required for living close to people (paragraph 22).

### Was the Council Responsible for the Serious Crisis Facing the Priesthood?

First of all, what exactly do we mean by the word "crisis"? A distinction must be made between crisis as a manifestation of decadence, and crisis as a sign of growth (or an opportunity that *allows* for new growth).

Ten years after the Second Vatican Council, a Spanish-born priest who had served in Latin America wrote, under my direction, a doctoral dissertation on the undeniable crisis in priestly life. He concluded that this crisis could very well turn out to be a crisis of growth, if priestly formation and spirituality are understood and developed within the framework of the Council's Pastoral Constitution *Gaudium et spes*. He also concluded that one of the major reasons for the seriousness of the crisis was precisely that this form of spiritual renewal was frequently neglected, if not explicitly rejected.

The dynamic acceleration of history in our age is unquestioningly enormous and unique. Most Church authorities are ill-prepared spiritually and theologically to fully realize the depth and strength of this challenge facing the Church today. It is especially those promoters of the Restoration "movement," forever harking back to antiquity and blaming the Council for this crisis and unrest, who are unable, if not unwilling, to realize and address the threat and opportunity presented in our rapidly changing history. They remain impregnated with, and ossified by, a timeless, classicist philosophy and theology that render all things changeless. They appear unable or unwilling to shift from a moralistic paradigm of obedience to an ethic of responsibility and co-responsibility. This lack of preparedness is even more visible in their clinging to centralism that overdoses on control in direct opposition to a genuine and more humane collegiality and subsidiarity. In an age of accelerated historical development and change, the trend and temptation to restore centralism and all systems of control may well be a major cause for completely missing or blocking opportunities to respond to ecumenism and global diversity through inculturation.

Those who should be giving an encouraging green light to promoting the shift to this new paradigm are instead putting the brakes on it. An obvious symbol of this aspect of the crisis is the cruel reality that even moderately dynamic bishops are regularly and punctually replaced when they have reached the age of retirement, while vigorous "brakemen" remain in office much longer. Bishops pioneering a contemporary outlook run the risk of being removed, while those lagging behind remain entrenched. While nostalgia for "the good old days" was far less dangerous in a more static era, today's yearning to turn the clock back may ultimately lead stragglers to suffer the fate of Lot's wife and risk becoming pillars of salt.

### Focusing on Encouraging Examples

Given the present state of the Church, like Galileo, we can trustfully say, *E pur si muove* (Yet there is movement). I could very easily write a well-documented book in support of my findings. As a German priest, I have chosen to refer to the letter of the German bishops to priests entitled "On the Priestly Ministry" (September 24, 1992). The document is a superb example of the paradigm shift taking place in our age.

With astonishing frankness and newness, the German bishops addressed the present crisis in the priesthood and invited its members as brothers, first and foremost, to open their eyes to positive opportunities, rather than wasting their best energies on useless moaning and groaning about how bad things are. Implied, of course, was that the darker sides of the priesthood—and the real dangers to it— should be neither minimized nor overlooked. Above all, it is a matter of priority, since the Christian spirit never points to the victory of evil first, and then only grudgingly turns to acceptance of the fact that God plays a role in sometimes granting victory to the good.

As bishops of the universal Church, the German leaders invited their fellow priests to develop a worldwide outlook, since the present crisis (hopefully a crisis of growth) is related to the deep transformation of cultures, societies, the sciences, and not in the least, the vision of the cosmos—the entire created world. Consequently, the relationship between Church and world can never again be the same. The era of Christendom has unequivocally and irretrievably passed away.

Priests stand uniquely in the midst of this crisis that for many is a crisis of faith. What does it really mean to abide in faith? In life and ministry, priests in particular (though vowed religious men and women and the whole people of God as well) are confronted with many paralyzing forms of polarization in the Church. On this point, the German bishops, with unwavering honesty, spoke about problems caused by current official Roman teachings on several aspects of sexual morality and marriage: teachings that are either simply overlooked or explicitly rejected by a great number of believers. As a consequence, two loyalties are in conflict. On the one hand, most priests have deep feelings of loyalty for the magisterium and the pope; and on the other hand, they intend to be faithful to the whole people of God. How are we to reconcile these opposites in terms of consciences and in pastoral teaching and practice? Who in this case suffers more than priests and pastoral associates?

This polarization is particularly painful for older priests whose formation has been substantially pre-conciliar. Not infrequently, the depth of this crisis even approaches the level of an identity crisis.

The German bishops' letter offers these challenging words,

in full realization of the problem: "The pastor bears with great suffering the final responsibility for the parish. But often he comes to see that many times lay people are more competent" (p. 5). The process of learning cooperation with lay people and younger priests is indeed not easy for all involved.

In confronting the problem of celibacy, the bishops are equally forthright when they ask: "Is the lifestyle marked by celibacy so important as to allow postponing what belongs to the very heart of pastoral ministry, at least as it has been conceived up until now?" (p. 6).

The bishops touch upon a number of problems in facing the question as to how the present crisis in the priesthood "coincides with the future image of the Church" (p. 9). In pondering the dynamics of our most recent history, the bishops conclude that now and in the future, even more than in the past, priestly vocations need to be understood and fostered in a *dynamic* way: "In the course of the years we have to truly become what we already are" (p. 10). Implied in this axiom is a challenging truth. A static vision of the priestly calling is deadly. They add further: "In this regard as in many others, we have to learn to accept and develop an approximate and gradual maturation" (p. 10). The dynamics of growth must increasingly characterize and be evident in priestly life, coupled with the courage to live a fully transparent life in face of the community—regardless of personal shortcomings (p. 13).

Conscientiously accepting our human imperfections and limitations can become an act of praise for God's generosity and patience. Simultaneously, this acceptance can be a remedy against the temptation to take ourselves too seriously.

In the vision of the German bishops, the present situation is both an invitation and a timely opportunity for priests, in solidarity with each other, to get on the road and place themselves in the midst of human need and affliction (p. 34). In my opinion, this new tone and spirit is poignantly revealed in their compassionate and timely directive: "At this point, we remind ourselves of our solidarity with those of our peers who, frequently under tragic circumstances, have left the ministry. In no way may we abandon them" (p. 30). Indeed the entire letter glows with the spirit of the Gospel and strengthens our hope for the future of the Church and the future of her priesthood.

The same pastoral tone of frankness and openness shines forth in the pastoral letter of Bishops Lehman of Mainz, Saier of Freiburg, and Casper of Rottenburg-Stuttgart on pastoral care for divorced and remarried Catholics—including the admission of the Catholics to the Eucharist in accordance with wise principles of discernment. Even after the disappointing response from the Vatican congregation on doctrine, these three bishops, in a spirit of nonviolence, maintain their spirit of candor and sincerity.

Only in mutual solidarity and trust between bishops and priests can the present and undeniable crisis be overcome, for what unites them is their shared love and pastoral care.

## CHAPTER 9

# PROGNOSIS FOR THE FUTURE OF PRIESTLY VOCATIONS

The question about the future of priestly vocations can be extremely painful if the discussion totally centers around the dearth of priests, without giving critical attention to the signs of the times and to the basic vocation of all Christians. Such a perspective is too narrow, even harmful for the mission of the Church. Therefore, I insist that we must dare to take a new look at the all-embracing Christian vocation, specifically in the light of Jesus' baptism in the Jordan by John.

### *A Thoroughly New Vision*

The vocation of Christ to which we are called is, first and foremost, the vocation of the nonviolent Servant of Yahweh for the salvation and peace of the world. Jesus' public life announcing the glad tidings of his passion, death, and Resurrection is programmed by his relationship with, and call of, his Father: "You are my beloved Son" (Mark 1:11). Jesus is called and anointed to bear the full burden of humankind in saving solidarity, in order to free humanity from destructive sin-solidarity. He is the prophet who goes ahead of us, showing us the way of peace, nonviolence, and the power of that love that aims at transforming enemies into friends.

Immediately after the baptismal event, the Gospel of Matthew offers us one of the main keys for understanding the drama of salvation. It does this by unmasking the most satanic temptations, by illuminating the false expectations of a powerful, violent Messiah, and by exposing the abuses of religion for earthly profit, power, and self-exaltation. Though temptations surround Jesus on every side, they have absolutely no power over him. It is for our sake that Jesus has, once and for all, unmasked them through absolute faithfulness to his calling as the suffering, nonviolent Servant-Son of God.

Mainly this understanding is a matter of approaching our Christian calling in light of Jesus' vocation. Therefore, it should be evident that the future of all Christian vocations depends upon how thoroughly faithful we are in following in the footsteps of the Servant of Yahweh in this new context. From the Constantinian era almost to the present time, most people were Christians *by birth*. Now the new paradigm ever more clearly urges us to be and become Christian by choice, by vocation. It implies that the future of the Church will be marked not only by particular "vocations," but especially by those who consciously make a personal choice to follow Christ, the nonviolent Servant of God. The difference between those who consciously and convincingly live the norm of Jesus' baptism in the Jordan in spirit and in blood and, on the other hand, those particular "cradle Catholics" who are more or less passive followers is much more relevant than the difference between the ministerial and universal priesthood. What really characterizes Christians is the depth of their understanding of what it means to be called in and by Christ to serve the cause of the kingdom of the Servant of Yahweh, and their firmness in embracing this all-encompassing vocation.

This basic vision is the solid ground for all Christian vocations, including the priestly life in the stricter sense. This is not a completely new idea. My parents, who were Christians by birth, became, in the course of their lives, even more so by choice, and while they especially lived out their calling as spouses and parents, they also were creatively committed to the life of the Church. They were farmers in the sight of the Creator, friends of the poor, and in no less equal measure, they faced enormous danger in their firm and courageous resistance to Hitler's regime.

Robert Schuman, who with Alcide De Gaspari and Konrad Adenauer was one of the major builders of reconciliation in central Europe, at one time hovered between the priestly life and professional politics. The priest who told him that he might fulfill his Christian calling in politics more than in the ministerial priesthood has rendered great service to the Church and the world. As a young professor, I had the good fortune of knowing De Gaspari and his family. With awesome simplicity, he served me in the celebration of Mass on many occasions. These were astonishing men who fulfilled their Christian calling in keeping with the testimony of the nonviolent Servant of Yahweh.

In no way do I mean to belittle the priestly calling, having had so many reasons to be grateful for it; but I dare say that the future of the Church and priestly vocations depends on a radical shift from the Constantinian paradigm to that of a freely chosen Christian vocation—one that avoids, at all costs, any thoughts of superiority. Such a shift will, of necessity, mean a new look at the vocation to the ministerial priesthood. There will be a sufficient number of priestly vocations if the main focus is on vocation in a much broader but more specific Christian sense, and always in view of the salvation of the world.

What a blessing it is to meet medical doctors and all kinds of therapists who, in a convincing way, embody the Christian vocation as healers and, at the same time, give witness to Christ the Healer! Similarly, can we not also look to lawyers who wisely work to create more humane laws and better application of them and who, through their profession, point to Christ, who did not come to judge but to heal?

I think here of one of my former students who enthusiastically studied theology but did not feel called to celibacy. As a juvenile-court judge, he developed a marvelous and creative capacity for healing. Instead of sending troublesome youths to prison, he offered them therapeutic opportunities to change their lives for the better by serving the community. For example, these young people were required to visit the sick and the elderly, at times bringing them flowers and also asking how they might render service to them. These young people were prohibited from telling those they visited that they were required by law to do this as reparation for their wrongdoing, especially since the judge did not impose these sanctions for the sake of punishment.

A book could be written on various vocations and the variety of ways in which people could live out their Christian calling for the salvation of the world, and in a manner in which the new paradigm "Christian by vocation" takes on flesh and blood. I have no fear that such a vision might be to the detriment of the specifically priestly vocation. To the contrary, I believe it would greatly enhance its authenticity.

## Should the Church Acknowledge the Sacramentality of Diverse Ministerial Vocations?

By renewing the doctrine of the universal priesthood of the faithful, and by explicitly entrusting a diversity of Church apostolic activities to laywomen and laymen, the Second Vatican Council has made a very relevant and timely contribution to the question of vocations. All around the globe, although to different degrees and in various modalities, a new nonclerical "clergy" has emerged.

With great joy and trust in the future of the Church, I have observed this development, especially in Africa. Thousands of well-trained catechists and their admirably generous wives do practically all of the parish work, which includes catechesis, religious formation of adults, peace-making, community-building, care for the sick and poor, solemn and joyous celebration of baptism, and, on each Sunday, they celebrate the liturgy of the Word and preside over the communion service, to name but a few activities.

In the light of these outstanding contributions, my question is: should these people be required to make a long journey on foot or on bicycle to receive the pre-consecrated bread? From a legal standpoint, considering all they have done, they still do not share in the sacramentally constituted priesthood. Most of these men do not intend to be ordained deacons, since that would mean they must embrace celibacy should their spouses die. Moreover, how can this celibacy even be conceived of in present-day African culture?

They cannot celebrate the sacrament of anointing, which, in African culture, has deep significance. Personally, I see no dogmatic obstacles in changing this. Does not the whole life of Jesus and the mission of the Spirit tell the Church: "Be creative!"?

Never in the history of the entire Church have there been such great numbers of theologically trained and highly qualified men and women. At the present time, the Church has even more trained people than she had in all her previous eighteen hundred years combined. Why, then, should we bemoan a lack of Christian vocations in the Church?

Together with the present pope, we have for a long time fervently prayed for celibate priestly vocations. Many have given up this quest in the absence of answers to these reasonable queries and thoughts: Why do *we* tell the Holy Spirit that priests should be given to us only through the doorway of celibacy? Do we think the Holy Spirit is delighted when *we* churchmen determine the size of the eye of the needle through which the Spirit *is supposed* to pull through the desired and much-needed vocations? Is there anything more idolatrous than imposing human will on the Holy Spirit or boxing the Spirit into our narrow categories of thought? Had the apostles and their first successors acted similarly by imposing these kinds of prescriptions on the Holy Spirit, they would have had to leave their wives and, of even greater import, they would have had to leave nearly all the young Christian communities without the Eucharist.

I repeat: Celibacy, as a freely distributed charism of the Spirit, is a noble and gracious gift, but Church authorities must make a well-thought-out and thoroughly conscious choice between the fullest degree of faithfulness to the testament and mandate of Jesus—"Take and eat, and drink from the cup, all of you"—and mere human tradition. We must be reminded that churchmen can fall prey, not only to the dangers of verbal heresy, but also to the dangers of "heteropraxis." During the period of the Inquisition, the Church engaged in the horrific practices of the torture and burning of innocent women perceived as witches. Denouncing these grave practices without looking most carefully to the present is nothing short of pretension and cover-up.

Celibacy, a precious charism and witness to the kingdom of God, does not derive its value in numbers, but rather in being lived authentically. Nor is celibacy primarily understood as being under the dimension of law. To the contrary, more than anything else, it proclaims in the words of Paul: "You are no longer under law, but under grace" (Romans 6:14).

## The Ultimate Christian Vocation:
### Witnessing to Nonviolence

My thoughts here are written on the day after meeting a courageous woman at a large assembly of Pax Christi members. We spoke about the noble vocation of those who, out of faith in Jesus as the Servant of Yahweh, witness to nonviolence. Her personal story of anguish spoke strongly to me, a story I had earlier mentioned, but that is worthy of recall here. When her husband, a young sacristan, came to the conclusion that it was better for him to die at the hands of Hitler's regime than to participate in killing others in a clearly unjust war, his pastor and bishop gave him no support. To the contrary, they even tried to dissuade him with the argument that, in obedience to law, he must be ready to accept military service. His wife, however, fully supported him as a co-witness. The letters he wrote to her during his last days are very moving and challenging to all of us who profess to witness to the nonviolent love of the suffering Servant of God. In one letter, he said:

> Dearest spouse, there was no way to spare you this suffering on my behalf. How must our dear Redeemer have felt the deep sorrow of his mother in behalf of his passion! Jesus and Mary suffered out of love for us. I thank our Savior that he allows me to suffer and die out of love for him.

Mahatma Gandhi, who exemplified the spirit of nonviolence, created ashrams, houses for shared learning of nonviolence, especially in the spirit of the beatitudes. Was it not, therefore, expected that men like Gandhi and Martin Luther King, Jr., would face death as a seal of their calling and mission?

For the first time in history, we have the capacity to exterminate our living planet, either quickly through nuclear war or by the gradual erosion of all life forms through our ongoing personal and corporate sins of ecological irresponsibility. The world needs nothing more urgently than people such as this sacristan and his wife, Mahatma Gandhi, Martin Luther King, Jr., and Dorothy Day— all of whom took their vocations seriously. If strength and resolve to become radical witnesses to justice, peace, and nonviolence do not flow from our eucharistic celebrations, then we must fearfully and sadly conclude that far too many priestly and lay Christian vocations are not sufficiently authentic.

For me, this is an infinitely greater concern than the number of celibate priests. The more our worries and concerns become narrow and parochial, the less likely it is that we shall focus on essentials and on larger, more encompassing issues.

## What About Women and the Priesthood?

Rapidly changing historical events and processes are particularly evident in the newly developing identity and social roles of women. Shall the Church adapt to these changes or lag behind? In this age, the development of women is a timely and decisive test for the Church of her desire to be salt for the earth in human history and an important dimension of her ministry.

A patriarchal and artificial view of the Church created many serious problems. Only a few centuries ago, it seemed a miraculous thing that Saint Vincent de Paul obtained permission for religious women to leave the enclosure in order to serve the sick and poor without heavy interference and supervision by churchmen.

What is the status of women in the Church at the end of the second millennium? Women's experience is well ahead of the current vision of the institutional model of the Church. There are already hundreds, if not thousands, of gifted and creative women theologians, more than in all previous centuries combined. Still, the Vatican makes it difficult for women to obtain chairs in Catholic Church-sponsored universities, especially if they espouse a feminist critique and reconstruction of theological questions and issues, not to mention Church doctrines. In spite of this, women are already very influential in making inroads in those colleges not controlled by Rome and, even more so, on ecumenical theological faculties.

In various parts of the world, women are entrusted with a variety of very important pastoral roles and, in a practical way, they already share in many ecclesial roles. Many preach retreats and give workshops, even for priests who highly esteem them and appreciate their expertise.

At parish levels, many are pastoral associates who, among a host of other responsibilities, console and bring communion to the sick. Even more, they empower the laity by forming and training lay pastoral-care teams to carry on the ministry to the sick, a ministry that goes well beyond initial hospital visits. They organize and educate lay social-justice teams aimed at raising parish consciousness and involvement in wider social issues that especially affect the poor and the oppressed. Women develop and foster Bible study groups in parishes and in homes for the purposes of deepening lay understanding of the Scriptures, especially as a source for spiritual development, and for helping lay persons to discover and act upon their Christian calling. All these things are being done in parishes where collaborative, pastoral leadership is the norm; that is, where pastors, having few ego needs, resist the temptation to control by refusing to engage in the exercise of power *over* others. Rather, the collaborative pastor shares the power of the Holy Spirit *with* others in recognizing, encouraging, and utilizing the wealth of talents and gifts of a well-educated faithful today.

Can women celebrate the sacrament of reconciliation? Many serve, in their lives and ministries, as sacramental signs of peace and reconciliation. Women are gifted with a special charism for generous forgiveness, and with a tremendous ability to relate wholesomely and most helpfully to the sick, elderly, and dying. In fact, women are an inspiration to others in more ways than have been presented here. I personally know a number of truly charismatic women whom bishops have appointed as hospital chaplains. Of course, we have yet to see a woman seated in the confessional waiting for penitents. Nonetheless, sick and healthy people—in their need and desire for repentance and reconciliation—have continued to trust and open their consciences to caring women.

In this regard, I will mention two significant examples from my experience. After World War II, a hospital for Nazi soldiers who were American prisoners of war was set up here in Gars, where I presently live. A number of these hardened men felt the need to tell their sins and even the crimes they committed during the war to a sister who cared for them. Praying with them, she taught them to bring their pain and sorrow before God in humble, trustful prayer. I cannot help but think that what happened there was indeed a sacramental moment much more profound than those confessions heard by harsh and ritualistic priests.

Another example is that of an older sister who, appointed as a hospital chaplain, is considered to be most trustworthy. Many patients spontaneously opened themselves to her and confessed what they considered to be serious sins. Unfortunately, there is a problem here. Patients had talked about a local priest who came to the hospital weekly or bi-monthly, anxiously inquiring about the number and species of their sins. Now, if the sister-chaplain had told her patients that they must confess to a priest—a requirement that, in many cases, would have meant confession to this unloved priest—a bad reaction would not have been uncommon. Patients either became angry, refused to confess, or, worse, became further alienated in attempting confession to him.

The question is not: "Can a woman celebrate the rite of reconciliation?" In our present circumstance, she does not offer herself to that rite. I know only of what women do in these situations. They listen to patients, pray with them, and praise God for his generous forgiveness, hoping and pleading for a sign of gratitude in patients' hearts that will lead them, in the future, to be forgiving toward those who have offended them.

Can women celebrate the sacrament of anointing the sick? While they do not at present, Church authorities could surely entrust them with this mission. I know a very gracious and much-loved sister who, with blessed oil, anoints the sick if asked, and prays over them. However, she does not use the liturgically prescribed formulas. Does she administer the sacrament? Formally speaking, no, but her radiant presence and inspirational anointing may very well be more grace-filled than in the case of the priest who rushes into a room, sacramentally anoints the patient, and then rushes out.

According to the "definitive" doctrine of Pope John Paul II, women can never celebrate as presiders at the Eucharist or, more technically speaking, never consecrate. Still, the successor of John

Paul II might well feel he is not bound by such a declaration, should he listen more patiently, not only to qualified and reliable theologians, but also to the common sense of the faithful who, in their discussion of various questions, give evidence of their own process of growth and discernment.

I sometimes hear this question: How do you, then, explain how a priest in the state of mortal sin can validly consecrate, while a holy woman can never do so? To that I respond with a key question: What does it mean to consecrate? It is not we priests who consecrate, such that what was bread becomes the presence of Christ. This mystery takes place on the occasion of *epiklesis,* by the power of the Holy Spirit. Should the solemn calling of the Holy Spirit to "come upon these gifts and make them holy" not be spoken by a holy woman while, in fact, not-so-holy men do it? In my thinking, the greatest sinfulness does not make an ordained priest incapable of "consecrating" any more than a holy woman would automatically and necessarily be excluded. In other words, does the sheer fact of being a woman constitute an insurmountable obstacle to validity, while the state of grave sin of a man would not? These are things we cannot bring together satisfactorily.

One thing today that is generally agreed upon is that Church authorities can offer no good reason whatsoever for excluding women from all the major processes and decisions relating as much to women as to men. Before it can be definitively decided what ministries can be opened up to women, care should be given to invite women, a most creative half of the Church, to substantially participate in the processes involved in all major collegial decisions. Is it not significant that during the 1994 World Synod of Bishops, which took up the issue of consecrated life, one bishop suggested that women should also participate in the election of the pope?

Regarding the issue of women's ordination, it has been sufficiently documented that the traditional argument against it is not only faulty but shameful, to say nothing of being theologically dangerous. The document *Inter Insigniores* (October 15, 1976) from the papacy of Paul VI refers to a number of medieval, rather than contemporary, theologians, such as Bonaventure, Duns Scotus, and Durandus. All of these men produced the same double (and doubly false) argument. Scotus' view is particularly "clear" if not downright odious:

> Order is a certain grade of eminence over others in the Church and is for a certain act of superiority which must somehow be signified by natural eminence of condition and rank. But woman is naturally in a state of subjection in relation to man, and therefore cannot possess a rank of eminence over any man....If she could receive Orders in the Church, she could preside and rule, which is against her condition....Hence she is not a matter capable of receiving this sacrament (Scotus, *In IV sent.* d. 25, *Scholion Opus Oxoniense*).

Thus, we can see how the male-superiority complex easily transfers itself into a priestly superiority complex, which, I might add, is a screaming contradiction to the central truth and image of Christ the *Servant*. It also becomes clear that the whole matter of ordination of women cannot truly be resolved as long as the Catholic priesthood is theoretically and practically understood as a state of lived superiority. A one-sided hierarchical and patriarchal thought pattern tends also to exclude women in the Church from all major decision processes. (See Dennis Michael Ferrara, "The Ordination of Women: Tradition and Meaning," *Theological Studies* 55 [1994]: 706-719.)

### Requisites for Presiding at the Eucharistic Celebration

Christ has instituted the Eucharist as a particularly loving gift for the pilgrim Church for all times and in all places. It seems to me that, from this basic truth, it is easy to draw the conclusion that any kind of prerequisite that would practically deprive Christian communities of the regular celebration of the Eucharist cannot be upheld and maintained.

This is a grave and binding truth for those in authority. Note that the Catechism of the Catholic Church states:

> The Sunday celebration of the Lord's Day and his Eucharist is at the heart of the Church's life (2177). The Sunday Eucharist is the foundation and confirmation of all Christian practice. For this reason the faithful are obliged to participate in the Eucharist on days of obligation unless excused for a serious reason. Those who deliberately fail this obligation commit a grave sin (2181).

In a moral theology meant not only for those *under* authority, but equally and especially for those *in* authority, it seems quite clear that Church leaders who create so many specific man-made conditions that hinder a great number of Christian communities and persons from regularly participating in the Eucharist, "commit a grave sin" (see above: 2181). For should it not be said that Church authorities themselves commit as many sins through their mandates that deprive people of the Eucharist? The point of departure for further deliberation might well be the meal communities of the early Christian Church.

## A Heartfelt Thanks to Worker Priests

Without a doubt, worker priests deserve our deepest gratitude. They were and are courageous pioneers in exploring new horizons for a better understanding of the inculturation of the ministerial priesthood. Metaphorically speaking, theirs was a tremendous leap over a deep and wide ditch. Priests and bishops known for their pastoral zeal and charismatic clairvoyance creatively dared to face the burning issue of alienation of the blue-collar working class from a Church that not only trailed behind history, but equally lagged behind the Gospel of "God with us"—Emmanuel. These priests acknowledged that scandal was created in losing contact with the worker class, just as today many alert Christians are afraid the Church might lose many of her best and gifted women.

The encyclicals of Leo XIII and Pius XI on the social question of the worker class were certainly examples of a step in the right direction, but they could not fill the abyss between Church practice and the culture of the working class. The world of Church and the world of workers appeared to be two disparate spheres. In France and Germany, bishops began to delegate able priests to primarily or exclusively serve the worker class. Paul Gauthier, as one among other more pastorally alert priests, had the common sense and courage to express it simply in these words: "France has become a mission country." Yet, in spite of all goodwill, priests sent to the working class were already marked by their identification with a different culture and class—that of the Tridentine priesthood, symbolized by the cassock. Most priests were simply unable to realize the depth of cultural difference and estrangement. We need not clarify here by speaking of the estrangement of the worker or that of the Church, since both were true.

It was the great Cardinal Emmanuel Suhard, with his counselors and chaplains of Catholic youth, such as Jacques Loew, OP, Henri Godin, and Yves Daniel, who took the initiative, the latter two of whom authored the shocking book *France, Mission Country?*

During the preparation for the Council, I had the opportunity of contacting and cooperating with Jacques Loew and Bishop A. Ancel, who was, himself, a worker priest, even as bishop. These were all wonderfully evangelical men who made a profound and abiding impression on me.

The reader may forgive a small excursion in recounting the following story told by Bishop Ancel, though it is very much to the point. After the solemn promulgation of the text *Veterum Sapientia,* promoted by the old men in the Curia—a text that stipulated that, in view of the forthcoming council, every effort should be made to perpetuate the "Latin culture" and, to that end, all philosophy and theology should forever be taught in Latin throughout the world,

Bishop Ancel, in the name of French bishops, went to the pope and frankly protested against it. Pope John was not surprised. He said, "Daily, I receive protests, and I understand why, but let me tell a story to explain this problem:

> Giorgio, a peasant living in the mountains over Bergamo, came to his bishop and asked him to make him a priest because all winter long, no priest had managed to come up to his little town, and so the people were without the Mass. He said, "I assure you that I can read the Latin Mass properly, although I do not understand the words. But I do understand what it means altogether." The bishop came to love the good man, but he told him, "Since you are a married man, I am not allowed to ordain you." A year later, Giorgio met the bishop again and said, "My holy wife, Margaret, has gone to heaven, and I don't intend to marry again. Now, can you ordain me?" Giorgio passed a short exam, and also showed how well he knew all the ceremonies, and so he was ordained. There was great joy in the village. Later, Giorgio came down to town for several days to celebrate in the cathedral. In the sacristy, all the other priests greeted him with "*Prosit!*" Giorgio asked an older priest what that meant. The priest, who was a scoundrel, said, "It is the greatest insult!" The next day, when Giorgio was again greeted in this manner, he became furious, and making a fist against the priests, responded in turn, "A *prosit* to you too!"

At that point, Pope John paused, pondered for a moment, then said to Bishop Ancel, "Did I only want that Giorgio should have been able to know the Latin word *Prosit*"? With a deep sigh, he confessed, "I hope that God will forgive me for this great fault of having yielded to the Curia."

Was not this cult of the Latin a symbol of alienation? At that time, a well-known cardinal wrote in the *Osservatore Romano* that Rome, for all times, had the duty to cultivate barbarians by the Latin "super-culture." In the same vein, Cardinal Giuseppe Pizzardo, then head of the Sacred Congregation of the Holy Office, in an attempt to suppress the worker-priest movement, offered his perspective:

belonging to the class of dependent workers is seemingly beneath the dignity of a priest. Why is it that this saintly old man could not come to the realization that vesting himself in purple and appropriating exotic titles was a glaring contrast to Jesus the carpenter?

In 1963, in the first year of his pontificate, Paul VI spoke to me about the worker-priest problem, revealing to me his deep understanding and pastoral solicitude. He provided me with a thick dossier and asked me to work out a memorandum on this burning issue for him. The decision of Paul VI to renew the "experiment" of worker priests found support and reinforcement in the Council document on "The Ministry and Life of Priests" (paragraph 8).

In spite of all pain and misunderstanding, the institution and final approval of worker priests was a signal of "opening windows" for a breath of fresh air. It has opened our eyes to an even wider problem—namely, the immense distance created by the formation and culture of priests shaped by the uni-forming Tridentine seminary, especially in its Roman type, which prevailed up to the time of Vatican II. It is the great task of the Church as a whole, but especially the task of her priests and bishops, to continue the process of inculturation in theology and ministry, so as to honor Jesus the carpenter, the "Son of Man," who is "one of us" in all things except sin.

The presence of worker priests, now almost all over the globe, is a sign of hope and of an ongoing challenge to the whole Church to aim for contemporaneousness with Jesus in the here and now of human history, as well as in all cultures. The key question for our quest is: "What kind of priests are needed for the Church and world?" It is this particular concern that has given me the courage and the impetus to write this small book.

### *Physically Challenged and Developmentally Disabled Priests*

Considering my present situation, I cannot help but think myself to be handicapped and physically challenged in various ways. Being larynx-ectomized is but one small symbol of my situation. From a larger standpoint, in looking to Emmanuel, the Word Incarnate, and also looking at the tremendous acceleration of history in our age, it can truthfully be said that we are all hampered and handicapped in both respects, lagging behind as we do to the nearness of Jesus to all his people and to the speedy course of our current history.

We priests today are deeply marked by the wounds that date not only from the present time. On our weak shoulders, we also bear the heavy weight of Church history. If we allow ourselves to recognize and acknowledge our great woundedness, and our status of being retarded and handicapped in so many ways, our very deficiencies may very well turn out to be God's gracious blessing in disguise. We might very well become signs and symbols of the disfigured Servant of God. "Here is my servant, whom I uphold, / my chosen, / in whom my soul delights" (Isaiah 42:1). "Many were astonished at him / so marred was his appearance" (Isaiah 52:14). "He was despised and rejected by others; / a man of sufferings and acquainted with infirmity; and as one from whom others hide their faces" (Isaiah 53:3).

I made this meditation when I read about a Protestant pastor who, gravely handicapped, graciously and generously served people who were disabled in many ways. What a difference from the old code of canon law that forbade the ordination of men with serious bodily defects! Our overall situation would be well symbolized and much improved if the Church would invite priestly vocations from among these suffering people, especially to serve people with disabilities. The lives of handicapped priests would be symbolic reminders to us of the Suffering Servant of God in our midst.

## CHAPTER 10

# THE MORE OR LESS LOVELY ANIMALS IN THE ARK

While it is true that the Church has priests and bishops whom she deserves, an important question is: Do priests have the kind of Church they deserve? A hard question indeed! All of us, from the simplest Christian to the pope, are living beneficiaries of the treasures of the Church's history, but we are also heirs of her burdens as well—a point I have tried to make throughout this book. Ours is an ambiguous history, for we treasure in our hearts many happy memories intermixed with innumerable scars. With all this in mind, I turn now to the various types of priests in our Church, particularly since our original question of dealing with what type of priests the Church needs is directly related to what kind of Church we will have.

### Noah's Ark: Inspiration for the Priesthood

I will attempt here, with the reader's permission, to give image to the various kinds of priests who journey with the whole pilgrim people of God we call the Church. To that end, I will make use of the symbol of Noah's ark as our craft, particularly since it fore-shadows the ark of salvation wrought by Jesus Christ.

One day, Noah became weary and upset and tearfully address-ing himself to the Owner of the ark said, "Dear God, why did you imprison me in this ark with so many awesome and awful ani-mals—with these crazy apes, stinking swine and…? The list was very long. God listened with compassion and then, with great kind-ness, said, "My dear Noah, do not forget that this ark is your salva-tion here and now. Why not also save the lives of these more or less lovely animals?"

### The Rooster: A Combination of Pride and Vanity

Of the several priests we have met in our lifetime, some might have just as soon chosen the rooster as their patron. On the dung-hill of vanity, he sings of his glory and might: "Look at me. Listen to me, Lord! I am mighty in my domain. Yes, indeed, do tell the hens and chickens to listen and obey me, because it is for their own sake!"

There are indeed "beautiful" temptations to vanity, but even more, there are atrocious temptations to pride that can easily arise among the clergy, especially those of higher rank and title. I truly hope that our infinitely patient God humorously and lovingly tol-erates these ridiculously vain roosters. In fact, I am confident that God does put up with them, because if I, a mere mortal made in God's image, can laugh at these vanities, within certain modest limits, how much more so can God chuckle in good spirits? I find it so wonderful that there are other good passengers in the ark who assist us all in avoiding a false and mean-spirited humor to un-mask our hapless antics.

Even so, under scrutiny, it is not the aroma of sanctity that surrounds priests who opt for pride, but rather it is a stinking odor. In self-defense, they can easily fall prey to the dubious act of justi-fying and rationalizing their pride and self-righteousness. For example, are they not outstanding runners in the race to ever higher careers, while leaving other runners in the dust? Are they not also eminently competent in administration and organization of their respective "barnyards"? Do they not sternly assert, with divine right no less, that they have exclusive competence in teaching and governing, with titles to seal their gifts? Apart from all this prowess, do they not also strut around in an array of color, beauty, and splendor, worthy of their high dignity?

But the most salient question remains. What indeed are they doing in the ark of salvation? Is it not by unrestrained humility that God, through Jesus Christ, enfleshed and made visible the plan of salvation? It is not God who has disproved all claims of the rooster-type priesthood? In the prayer of the humble Servant-maid Mary does not the Servant of God warn us all?: "He has scattered the proud in the thoughts of their hearts. / He has brought down the powerful from their thones, / and lifted up the lowly" (Luke 1:52).

Praise be to you, O God, for in your ark there are many unpretentious priests, bishops, and popes, alongside all your lonely, humble people—the *anawim*, who have heeded your words and have embodied the humble life of Jesus the carpenter. In their lowliness, you have revealed in them your true glory!

### The Nightingale

One of the most admired and beloved singers among the birds is the nightingale. I frequently listen to his sweet song in my early morning hours, though I have yet to catch a glimpse of one. The nightingale provides me with a meditation on one particular aspect of Christian and priestly authenticity. In an artful way, the nightingale both shields himself from the human eye and reveals himself in his nocturnal trilling of joyous praise. If we are the least bit reflective, this lovely Old World thrush can remind us of how important it is to develop an authentic priestly life that attracts people to the blissful message and praise of God, but does not draw attention to the messenger. The nightingale reminds us that there is no room for inflated egos that could potentially overshadow God's joyous, liberating message, or block it entirely from the ears of the faithful. The authentic priest is one who reveals his true self, by pointing others, not to himself, but to God. The authentic priest-messenger never stands in the way of the message. Essentially, this is the meaning of the Ignatian adage: Everything to the greater glory of God.

There is one experience I often call to mind that truly illustrates the vocation of the nightingale. In 1950, when I had the opportunity to preach a mission at a local parish, the pastor's housekeeper told me a remarkable story, in response to my glowing words about the good relationship between the elderly pastor and his young associate. Up until I met her, she had never revealed this story, because her pastor had sworn her to secrecy. Nonetheless, she decided to tell me, trusting that I would not make it known in the parish. So, this is the story of our nightingale:

After spending five years in the armed forces as a medical orderly in World War II, the young priest was appointed to the parish, and in no time at all, had won the hearts of all. Weary of this, the pastor missed no opportunity to remind the new associate that he, the pastor, was in charge. Wavering between jealousy and admiration, the pastor gradually sensed that he might very well learn something from his associate in serving his parish, which had a number of poor refugees.

One day, the young associate asked the housekeeper to make arrangements to have his own bed brought to the poorest family, which he had just visited. He also forbade her to tell anyone that this was his only bed. As it is not uncommon for misconceptions to occur when secrecy prevails, a story circulated among the parishioners that the pastor had sent a bed to a poor family for which, time and again, the people expressed their appreciation. The old man simply was unable to inform his parishioners that it was not his bed, but rather the gift of his associate. Still, he looked for an honorable solution and decided to give two of his surplus beds to the poorest in the parish. The overall result was a completely renewed relationship between the pastor and his associate whose love and simplicity was contagious, as well as a totally new relationship between the pastor and the parish. Moreover, the housekeeper added that she, too, greatly profited by this example and learned a great deal.

Had he known, I do believe that the young priest would have blamed the housekeeper for telling me this story, but I assured her that I would not spread it while I was there. However, in my ministry to other countries, I told this story to many priests, a story I tell myself time and again, because it is a classic story of a humble, self-effacing priest who has learned the art of self-concealment so that others may truly turn their full attention to the Lord and his Gospel.

## The Stern Moralist

On several occasions when I was invited to speak to a gathering, I was introduced to the gathering as "a great moralist." Filled with shame, I asked myself how did I come to deserve this insulting title, since most people understand the term "moralist" as having a negative connotation. A moralist is one who is forever judging and admonishing the faithful. He is always focused on indoctrinating them with all the "obligatory" prohibitive laws and precepts, with little or no regard for circumstances that might allow for exceptions, and coercing them through fear and damnation. So much for the development of moral maturity and virtuous character that far exceeds the limits of rules and blind obedience! Were this unholy moralism God's standard for salvation, the ark would be quickly evacuated, and hell would be overpopulated!

The typical moralist aims at completely controlling personal conscience, in part by demanding an accurate categorization of sins according to number and species. In the confessional setting, the priest-controller unconsciously makes the encounter a place of torture and excessive scrutiny, substantiated in these oft-asked questions: How many times have you committed the terrible sin of masturbation? How many times have you nurtured in your heart unchaste thoughts, and of what kind were they?

Thankfully, today's Catholics have learned to choose among confessors, and most can readily find priests who have learned from Saint Alphonse and others of his kind that the confessor's primary role is to be and become ever more the mirror image of the all-merciful God, an image of Jesus the healer, and that "judgment" (insofar as any human can judge) means, above all, the gift of discernment between what is genuine love and its counterfeit.

Happy the dwellers of the ark who, in contact with priests and other fellow Christians, not only experience the liberating power of God in the words of Saint Paul: "You are no longer under law, but under the grace of God" (Romans 6:14), but also, gifted as they are through the power of the Holy Spirit, help each other in an encouraging way. Be gone all you moralists, and do not return until you can learn from the humble of heart how to mediate the loving and compassionate forgiveness of your Creator!

### The Sentinel

To be a sentinel or guardian is, of itself, not a bad thing, if priests understand their service as a responsibility to protect the rights and liberties of all against unjust infringement. However, guardians of the faith can all too easily find pleasure in the power and exercise of control, especially if they have nabbed someone whom they believe has erred. Carried to an extreme, such priests will denounce a person for even the slightest transgression of a marginal law, often without ever testing the validity of the law itself.

Is it not puzzling that in our Church today, sons of guardians use their high positions to exercise excessive control over all matters of orthodoxy, especially nonrevealed doctrines, while, not so ironically, they are totally unable to convince even the most seriously committed Christians that these teachings come from God, not to mention exercising control over people on matters having nothing to do with orthodoxy? A system of near complete control arises from suspicion, and it creates an unholy and unhealthy climate for human relationships, which is irreconcilable with the primary mission of the Church to heal and not to judge.

In a culture with ever-increasing possibilities for manipulating the brain, public opinion, and the human genome, the burning question that comes to the fore is: Who controls the manipulators and controllers? Uncontrolled controllers can be likened to a devastating plague for which we must always be on guard.

We know from history that all totalitarian regimes, like those of Hitler and Stalin, fostered an ever-increasing system of clever and subtle controls. After the collapse of the Stalinist regime in East Germany, it was a tremendous shock to discover how many people were insidiously controlled by others at the uncontrolled top, and who, themselves, had become controllers in return. Is it not surprising, too, that many controllers were men of considerable reputation? Even prisoners in concentration camps were offered better living conditions, should they choose to control and denounce their fellow prisoners. In the end, almost everyone became prisoners of their own doing in some way by this refined and deceitful and traitorous system of control.

The Church on all levels must shy far away from such a system of control. Instead it would be hoped that the Church, in exercising her best wisdom, would endorse and find recourse in, coherent emphasis on the "reciprocity of consciences," which, practically speaking, means actively committing herself to fostering a healthy public opinion coupled with respectful dialogue.

Church authorities must never, in any way, concede to the temptation of voicing or accepting trends born of horrific ideologies such as we have experienced in this century. As a beacon of truth and light, the Church must always be on guard against such indiscriminate clichés as "My country right or wrong!" or, as was the case in Germany, "Hitler, the Führer, is always right!"

Moreover, a Church who professes to embody the justice and humility of Christ needs to be wary of her own ill-conceived and overly biased ideologies as well. In the process, every priest—be he pope, cardinal, bishop, pastor or associate—serves the Church well in gratefully accepting and acting on constructive criticism as a means to deeper understanding of truth. In this age, history should remind us all the more how very significant it is to develop and foster the virtue of critique, which essentially is holy discernment, wrought by theological reflection and shared experience. This virtue implies that we all, at every level of Church, accept and offer constructive critique to one another.

Embracing the vision of the Second Vatican Council can be a tremendously liberating experience and a marvelous opportunity for furthering the quest of ecumenism—particularly since Pope John XXIII has already paved the way for us by making major inroads through greater openness and honest dialogue.

The insistence of the Council in promoting collegiality and the development of structures for subsidiarity should prevail over tendencies toward centralism, authoritarianism, and retrenchment. The overriding mentality and practice of excessive control must be unmasked for what it is—an enemy of the freedom and creativity for which Christ has liberated us all and succinctly, the enemy of credibility and integrity.

One of the most important criteria for determining a genuine priestly vocation is a deep rootedness in, and practice of, the virtue of nonviolence. Prior to Vatican II, in some parts of the Church, there was in place a type of moral teaching based upon control for controller types that all too frequently cultivated a negative breed of priest-guardians. While I hope the controlling mentality has, for the betterment of the Church, enjoyed a happy death or, at the very least, is well on the wane, I still think it is important to provide at least two examples of this mentality as a warning for those who might still be lured to it.

After I returned from Russia in 1945, I preached a parish Advent mission. At the request of all the missionaries, I invited everyone, without exception, to come to confession or for discussion since, in the great and merciful generosity of Christ, all are invited to the sacrament of peace. Many people, including divorced and remarried spouses, courageously responded to this invitation. The pastor, on the other hand, made no effort to hide his anger toward me, being, as he said, "very preoccupied with discipline in the Church." One day, he not only denied a woman communion when she approached him, but he even spoke harshly to her, in full hearing range of the faithful.

At the dinner table, no longer able to contain himself, in no uncertain terms, he said to me, "You have given absolution to persons living a scandalous life" (meaning, of course, persons who were divorced and remarried). Just at that moment, the husband of the woman who had been refused the Eucharist walked in and told the pastor that his wife was, indeed, not a divorced woman. The husband insisted that the pastor make amends by asking forgiveness of the congregation for what he had done. That evening, the pastor even asked me to pardon him! The great wonder is that the shock of this experience turned out to be quite healthy for him.

During Lent, I was responsible for "hearing confessions" for three full days in another parish, where few would approach the pastor. As strange as this might seem to some readers, what subsequently happened reveals why it was so. One day, near the confessional, I saw this pastor slap a woman in the face. The woman came to me at once to complain that she had done nothing other than deliver a brief message to another woman in the church. In his own eyes, the pastor perceived himself as a pious man, fulfilling all his "religious duties." In conscience, he was driven, but the question remains as to what kind of conscience? There is little doubt that this pastor's view of the sentinel, in the service of the "discipline of the Church," issued from a misguided and misinformed conscience.

Poor priest-sentinel! Perhaps without guilt you have interiorized a kind of moral teaching and discipline that is both sick and sickening. Do not allow the thousands of man-made laws and prohibitive precepts based on a system of reinforcements to imprison you! In the depths of your soul, do you not feel ashamed of this slavery under law that infects you, and that in turn leads you to contaminate others, instead of leading them into the blessed freedom of the children of God? If you search among the faithful, whom you call lay women and lay men, you will find many competent healers, therapists, and other witnesses of joy and inner peace. Go to them, as they can surely help you!

Fortunately, the number of extremely scrupulous priests is decreasing, but there are still quite a number of younger extremists in the priesthood who have developed a fundamentalistic attitude, because they were taught to believe in law and discipline as though these were the zenith of their priesthood and of their ministry to others.

For sentinel-priests, controlled by law and discipline, celibacy is not a freeing experience insofar as it is misunderstood as part of a "holy system of law." For that reason, they lack the joyful experience of the charism of celibacy.

Among scrupulous and legalistic priests, there are many who are basically good and sincere, though misguided in having interiorized a faulty notion of what it means to be a guardian of truth. How much good they could have done, and could still do, were they open to being led by Christ and his true priestly followers into the promised land of creativity and authenticity, instead of clinging to the rails of law for power that provides a false sense of security!

As I earlier noted, some of us believe that many young men do long to serve God in the priesthood but dare not make the commitment, not only because they fear discovering down the road that they cannot live celibately but also because, even more, they fear being ousted from the priesthood in a humiliating manner. I have wept many times with priests who had sincerely made the commitment, men with precious human qualities, who were driven to despair by insensitive ecclesial policemen and guardians of law. Experiences of this kind become a counter-testimony to the joy of celibate life.

Still, I would not entirely exclude the sentinel from the ministerial priesthood if only this image were understood within the larger concept of "one of us." If priests of this type act in a perfectly nonviolent manner, they can become pioneers of a nonviolent culture. Unarmed and exemplary guardians of public order and freedom would clearly be a qualitative and cultural leap.

## The Ritualist

In the ark of salvation, the number of troubled and troubling ritualists has been considerably reduced. Some fifty years ago, ritualism was one of the major plagues in the Church. It was not uncommon to see priests, anguished over the issue of validity in the "administration" of the sacrament, sweating while pronouncing the words of consecration. Even highly gifted priests in important positions were plagued with doubt about their own ordination. Did they (as was then prescribed under pain of invalidation) touch the chalice, paten, and host simultaneously? Fortunately, Pius XII, as earlier noted, put an end to this tragic comedy by officially declaring that this rite was not a condition for valid orders.

Ritualism in any form can simultaneously become a humbling and self-exalting sickness. Being scrupulous, even with regard to the slightest ritual prescription, could become a form of self-assurance for a priest, rooted in unquestioning obedience and order. In that sense, ritualists can readily be transformed into watchdogs. Here is one example. As a young Redemptorist I stayed at one of our houses and asked the superior if, prior to my morning departure, I might celebrate the Mass. Cryptically, he warned, "If you dare!" After Mass, as I was hurrying to make the train, I was detained by an older peer who said, "Listen, Bernard, you have made two liturgical errors, and this is a grave matter for us." After listening to his two main points, I told him that there was no Church law about his concerns. In reply, he told me that a manual written by a Redemptorist made it quite clear, and that we must strictly conform to the order for the sake of unity.

Even though extreme cases of ritual scrupulosity and mean-spirited control have greatly diminished, ritualism still exists. Even among important churchmen, it remains a most serious obstacle to inculturation and liturgical spontaneity.

Does not the present law of celibacy, at least in part, aid and abet such a system of ritual purity to the detriment of the Lord's solemn mandate: "Do this, all of you, in memory of me!"? In other words, the man-made law of celibacy can, and has become in some situations, an obstacle to the divinely guaranteed right to the Eucharistic celebration of all the faithful.

### The Timid One

Poor fellow! Who has castrated you and deprived you of all creativity, courage, and enthusiasm? For centuries, the Church in Rome did castrate young boys in order to preserve the high pitch of their voices since women were not allowed to sing in the Church. In the first place, it was a terrible practice in itself and, second, it was done for all the wrong reasons. For me, this is just one more example of depriving priests of the gift of creativity and frankness.

Has not the timid priest, like everyone else, received from God a spirit of courage and truthfulness? The timid priest is one who has unfortunately interiorized a falsely sacralized, imposing, and frightening system of power. Instead of unmasking this kind of power for what it truly is, the timid priest, operating from a false sense of humility, tyrannizes others and, in the process, thwarts his own capacities for inner strength.

Overcoming timidity calls for an honest appraisal and a gathering together of inner resources, especially the recovery of an inborn tenderness. In so doing, priests and lay ministers can be healed and freed of their own self-oppression—a healing that can enable them to heal others. Vigilance is the virtue that alerts priests to the ways in which they could potentially contaminate others by wrongly imposing their false sense and practice of servile submission.

To the timid I say, let the Good News resound in your hearts, and the oil of gladness soothe your every pore to liberate you! Allow yourselves to receive the encouragement and consoling power of the Paraclete, and you will be blessed with fruitfulness! Pray fervently that the Holy Spirit may pour out upon you the gracious charisms of courage and joy that will enable you to console and encourage others! Make every effort to deepen your understanding of the biblical vision of *paraklesis,* for it is the Holy Spirit who is your Advocate before the Creator! It is the Spirit's liberating power that, if received openly, will free you *from* shyness and timidity, and will free you *for* joy, and fill you with the fire of franchise, the precious gift of the Spirit. It is the courageous and creative Spirit of Christ, the Prophet and Servant of Yahweh whom you are called to embody and serve, who impels you to nonviolence, freedom, trust, and inner strength.

### The Pessimist

To the seemingly less lovable creatures of the ark belong the incorrigible professional pessimists. They are an annoying downpour on all the others. Some are "prophets of doom" who constantly pester others, as John XXIII pointed out at the beginning of the Council. To our misfortune, sour pessimists are capable of negatively influencing the climate of the Church.

In those times when, around the Vatican, I encountered

sour-faced priests, clad in long cassocks trimmed with violet or otherwise, I often wondered to myself if there was anything that could be done to exhilarate them. Are there no places in the Church to therapeutically heal these men? Or, at least, are there not places where they could hide until they have, through the grace of God, overcome their pessimism, lest they contaminate others?

By vocation, priests are meant to be signs and witnesses to the joy of the redeemed. They are called to be a song of praise, a source of inspiration and hope, even should they have a fundamentally melancholic personality and disposition. Under favorable conditions, perhaps they could have become deeply contemplative Christians—some even gifted with mystical experience.

Other priests, however, have developed a pessimistic attitude because they have been overburdened with work and responsibilities beyond their resources, especially those in environments that overemphasize efficiency and success. Because of their specific natural proclivities, pessimists can more easily become deeply discouraged by hostile surroundings and unhealthy structures. Had they had the opportunity to live and work in a milieu marked by peace and joy, perhaps they could have become living fonts of peace and encouragement for many others. Under most unfavorable conditions, the good wine of their persons runs the risk of becoming vinegar. What a tragedy that would be!

The skunk is the symbol of the contagious pessimist. A beautiful animal to see, but woe to those nearby, if it feels threatened! On one occasion when I was in the United States, I visited my brother Martin, whose beautiful house was surrounded by an infernal odor. He said to me, "I saw a skunk near the house and, unfortunately, I tried to drive it away; irritated by my action, he left me the entire wealth of his skunkiness. Now we have to wait for the rainy season before we can hope to be rid of this terrible smell."

Perhaps, were the skunk able to pray, he just might do so in this way: "God of all creatures, including me, in spite of my undeniable beauty, people just don't like me. Why have you given me this most effective weapon of self-defense that so readily drives people away from me and forces me into isolation? What kind of identity crisis shall I have to undergo when, in the kingdom, I shall be rid of my stench?"

Who knows? Perhaps a pessimist who reads this prayer might come to recognize himself more fully, and take it upon himself to make a change along the way.

## The Clown

Recently, I read in the press how groups of clowns regularly and without pay visit hospital children's wards. These clowns, who have an enormous capacity for joy, wonderfully infect children with their humor. Doctors tell us that clowning aids the healing process, especially those who have psychosomatic illnesses. I personally know a charming clown, the father of three children, who could easily secure a good position as a college professor. Instead, he chooses to be a clown and radiates humor everywhere. Unquestioningly, he exudes, in my view, an overwhelmingly optimistic view of life and of the world. For me, the clown comes closest to the priestly vocation. Could not others like my friend, who has the lovable and wholesome heart of the clown, be missioned by the Church to pastor other clowns, their families, friends, and especially those who are ill and in need of the oil of gladness?

There was a time when wise kings employed court jesters. These wise fools were given the privilege of saying whatever they liked, in a humorous and often zany way, for the purpose of unmasking bad attitudes and dangerous trends in the realm. In this sense, the king understood something of what it means to give an advance of trust, knowing full well that it was ultimately for his own benefit. On the surface, it was pure jest, but underneath there was usually an insightful message. The "dead-serious humor" of the court jester often served to blame or warn the king and his cohorts about their own foibles and failings, a very valuable contribution to the stability of the monarchy should the king be so wise as to listen and take heed.

On one level, the act of clowning can be an act of protest against all wrongdoing; and on another, it can proclaim the Good News that things can change for the better, as long as we are wise enough, like the king, to open our ears to listen and our eyes to see. I do not think I am alone in support of the need for a few dead-serious, humorous clowns in the Vatican and elsewhere. They would greatly contribute to making such places more attractive, congenial, and wholesomely constructive milieus. Gentle, loving clowns deserve our utmost gratitude, since they not only make us laugh, but also propitiously warn us not to take ourselves too seriously. A Church that does not appreciate laughter and a profound sense of humor is, in my eyes, not very serious, in the true sense of the word.

### The Musician

In the story of Noah's ark, we are reminded that God has lovingly saved thousands of species of singing birds and flying insects who not only contribute to the ecosystem on which we depend for our livelihood, but who seem also to live to delight us with their music, showing us how to communicate joy in living together.

Should priests not be, in every fiber of their being, joyful musicians who sing and enable others to sing the praises of God? Indeed should not all of us who profess to be Christian sing and play together before the Creator of all harmony? The outward expression of joy and the sharing of it in the Lord mutually reinforce each other in the best sense. All the earth should resound to the heavens with hymns and songs of mutual love as a response to the great unstinting love of God. The Gospel and all of creation, themselves songs of love and beauty, should enchant us evermore.

There were times when, because of a particular emphasis on priests' singing in liturgy, only the well-trained could be ordained.

Thankfully, I escaped that requirement. Otherwise, I might have had some trouble. Nonetheless, tuneless as I am today, I still very much love music. The music of Beethoven, Mozart, Handel, and Bach offer me profound inspiration because these works, not unlike more specifically liturgical music today, ultimately issue from and express the creative heart of God. Music is good news and good prayer that never fails to interiorly uplift me.

My point here is simply this: priests should be persons who, in the totality of their lives, are truly songs of praise, inviting others to the never-ending praise of God. Regardless of what might happen in life, we always have thousands of reasons to rejoice in songs of praise and gratitude to God.

### *The Healer*

In many religions, especially in the so-called "primitive" religions, the priest and healer are coexistent, be it woman or man. Holiness derives its meaning from the word *wholeness*, and consequently the two terms are closely interrelated. In an unsurpassable way, Jesus Christ is simultaneously the Revealer and Healer—the perfect Adorer of God, and the unique Savior and Healer of all humankind and of all creation.

By his very presence and his supreme qualities of love, kindness, gentleness, by the inspiring trust and hope that marked his relationships, Jesus radiated and communicated health in every sense of the word. He healed in such a way that the healed praised God and brought hope to others in turn. In the totality of his person, Jesus is, in an unconditional way, the living Gospel of healing.

While not all priests need be well-trained therapists, much less medical doctors, they should have developed deeper insight into what constitutes human health and wholeness, as well as an understanding of what fosters health and wholesome relationships.

Moral theologians especially have the task of testing all moral thought and teaching to see if they promote sanity, health, and healing, while ever reflecting true images of God. Canonists, as well, are entrusted with the important healing and moral mission to test canon law in its development and self-understanding, and to see if it promotes healing, healthy structures, and relationships in every way. Moreover, canonists have the responsibility to warn against any use of law to create mutual distrust, superiority complexes, and other negative consequences.

In the choice of potential candidates for the priesthood, proportionate attention must be given to overall psychological health and to the candidates' capacities for cultivating and inspiring trusting human relationships. What is needed are priests and seminarians filled with joy in the Lord and gifted with a joyful heart, expressed in love for all persons. These are our true healers, even if they do not always explicitly reflect it in the course of their ministry.

### The Prophet

Good priests do not automatically have the charism to decipher future events, but in union with the faithful, they certainly must try to learn how to interpret the "signs of the times." This can be done by continually focusing, first and foremost, on the encouraging signs of the presence of God and, then, in right proportion, by attending to the alarming signs. Those who give primary attention to what is going wrong can easily degenerate into "prophets of doom," which is in plain opposition to the priestly task of proclaiming the glad tidings of the Saving Christ.

Prophetic persons have a vision of wholeness, and they do not get caught up in the web of small details. They are persons who discern present events, express gratitude for the good of the past, and take on responsibility for the future. Above all, the prophetic among us are those who are watchfully ready to embrace new opportunities (*kairos* moments) that offer hope for human betterment. They in no way tolerate the unholy union of "if" and "but." It is their very conformity to the Saving power of God that gives them a peculiar clear-sightedness for what is happening in the here and now and for what must be done. They share their vision of wholeness and inspire others by their creativity.

Prophets in every age have shaken up our personal and collective consciences by unmasking hidden and subtle temptations. However, the charism of revealing what is evil and dangerous prospers only to the degree that this gift is firmly rooted in grateful acceptance for all the good offered to us, which can also be replicated by us.

### The Saintly Penitent

In the ark of salvation, Peter is surrounded by saintly penitents whom he deeply reveres. Many have sinned to a lesser degree than he, and Peter himself would likely say they have exceeded him in humility and in doing penance as well.

Karl Rahner tells us that the Church is holy insofar as she is a saintly *penitent*. This also extends to priests. If we are self-righteous and self-satisfied with our priestly achievements, we remain on the dunghill of vanity, and the cock's crowing at Peter, prior to his conversion, crows for us too.

The growing number of priests who have sinned against chastity today has caused the Church great suffering and has, in many cases, created scandal among believers and nonbelievers alike. For example, the unmasking of pedophilia today has not only hurt victims of abuse, which must not be minimized, but also good priests who pay the price of scrutiny as well. Still, I wish to encourage priests who have failed in chastity, whatever the sin or abuse, by pointing out a few examples of saintly penitents who can serve as models for them. Also, let us never forget that as terrible as sins against chastity are, there are other sins that are no less grave and no less damaging, which, in the main, should awaken and alert us all to the need for lifelong conversion.

In the days when all diocesan priests were obliged by the force of law to make a retreat at least once every two years, one priest came to me and asked, "What sense does it make for me to confess my sins when I know I am an absolutely hopeless case? I have committed every possible sin against the sixth commandment!" We had a good and long conversation. I concluded that if he simply aimed at law-abiding mediocrity, I had little hope for him. On the other hand, I said, "You do have another choice. You could become a saint." He was astounded, and after shedding many tears said, "With God's help, I shall try." Over the years, he kept contact with me, and as it turned out, by the grace of God, he radically changed his life. Time and again, he wrote these words to me: "Yes, it does work, as long as I courageously try to live the life of a saintly penitent." In our discussions, we had, of course, earnestly looked at the ways becoming a saintly penitent could be realized in daily life. Years later, this priest urged me to heed his words: "You should tell this challenging truth which has changed my life to all who are in similar straits." Here, I tell it.

Another time, I visited a priest who had been sentenced to two years in prison for perjury. Under oath, he had denied that he had sired a child in an adulterous relationship. For him, I offered this message of hope: "Make up your mind! You can become a saint. However there can be no hope for even a level of correctness, if you merely aim for mediocrity." During his incarceration, because of his humility and kindness, he truly became an apostle to his fellow prisoners. Later, he was given a pastorate abroad, and the bishop of that diocese, in full recognition of what had happened, gave him another chance. Years later, I had the opportunity of meeting some of his parishioners, who, not knowing his past, said that they were given a saintly pastor, a humble and kind man of prayer, who lived a simple lifestyle in a radical way.

All those priests, who in the eyes of many are perceived as nothing more than failures, God's gracious presence and strength are always offered them, should they resolve to accept these gifts and strive to become saintly penitents. If they can honestly choose to make a radical decision to change their lives, and if, in the process, they are helped by a hope-inspiring friend, they may indeed succeed. Moreover, in their struggle for greater wholeness, they convey, to all of us, the profound truth that the Church is holy only to the degree that her members are saintly penitents.

I also recall other priests in which the firm determination to strive for the life of a holy penitent led them to humbly decide to return to the lay state. Only God knows the great number of so called "ex-priests" who have become outstanding examples of humility and zeal.

## CHAPTER 11

# BEHOLD THE HANDMAID OF THE LORD

It is much more than mere sentiment or devotional embellishment that I conclude this book by turning my full attention to Mary. In a unique way, Mary stands at the side of Christ the Servant of Yahweh, she who, in her response to God's offer, said, "Here am I, the servant of the Lord" (Luke 1:38). Does not her word indicate that Mary (whom the Church calls "Blessed Virgin") understood, in a developmental way, her own role of being present to Jesus in light of the four Servant songs?

### Mary: Servant of God and Model for the Priesthood

With Joseph, can we not assume that Mary sang into the heart of her child the self-same Servant songs of her Jewish heritage that nourished her own deep faith? Hers was an expectation totally opposite to that of the Jewish high priests who, missing the real message of their scripture, anticipated a powerful Messiah brandishing a sword. Mary's faith was that of the *anawim*, the humble people of

Israel who, with unwavering hope, unceasingly sang and prayed for a nonviolent, humble Servant who would set them free—a deep hope awakened in them by the inspiring words of Second Isaiah. Mary was the privileged maiden chosen to be for her son, Jesus, the total embodiment of this hope.

Mary, as the humble servant of Yahweh (as she even describes herself in the decisive hour), comes closest to the mystery and mission of Christ, mightily revealed from the outset of his baptism in the Jordan, brought to completion in the baptism of his blood on the cross, and finally sealed by his Resurrection.

Perhaps at this point, a word should be said about the traditional doctrine that asserts that the rite of priestly ordination imprints an indelible mark on the soul of the priest—a doctrine, I might add, which has nothing to do with magical concepts or literalism. From Mary's standpoint, we can truly say that she was the mirror image of her son in an embodied way, marked and sealed as she was by her calling to be a servant of the Lord. It is by the power of the Holy Spirit that she is "baptized" and consecrated to serve the unique "Servant of the Lord," as a nonviolent suffering servant to the honor of God, for the salvation of humankind and of all creation. Thus, we can conclude that she is a major participant in the victorious eschatological battle against the spirit of arrogance and violence. If my interpretation of the indelible character of the priesthood, as also revealed in Mary's role, is correct, I would hope that it would become a strong motivation for, and an essential perspective on, the priestly life in a totally tangible way.

Mary's role in the life of the Church is crystallized in her undivided presence to Christ in his suffering and death on the cross. We praise her because God "looked with favor on the lowliness of his servant / ...He has brought down the powerful from their thrones, / and lifted up the lowly" (Luke 1:48-52). The Magnificat, the longstanding prayer of the *anawim,* is not only a great prophetic word uttered by Mary. Rather, she *is* the Magnificat in the flesh, who, throughout her life, was present to Jesus, the Servant of Yahweh, in all the significant moments of his life.

At this point, it is helpful to return to the criteria Peter provided for the election of an apostle: One who "has accompanied us during all the time that the Lord Jesus went in and came out among us, beginning from the baptism of John until the day when he was taken up from us...as a witness with us to his resurrection" (Acts 1:21-22). More than all the apostles of her time and more than all fervent Christians in every age, Mary totally fulfilled the criteria for apostolic presence by birthing Jesus in poverty, presenting him at the Temple, sharing his exile in Egypt, rearing him into adulthood, and finally by standing beside him at the cross with John, the only other apostle present, Jesus entrusted both of them to each other.

Why does Scripture say nothing of appearances of the risen Christ to Mary, his mother? I consider the following explanation to be convincing: All the Gospel narratives on the Resurrection appearances focus mainly on the perspective of the need to gradually overcome despair and doubt among Jesus' followers. Mary, on the other hand, was privileged to immediately enter into the faith of Jesus' glorious Resurrection on the basis of her unique spiritual nearness to the Servant of Yahweh.

In his beautiful document *Marialis Cultus,* Paul VI himself pointed Mariology and devotions to Mary in the direction of this biblical understanding. The Magnificat is one of the unsurpassable prayers of a true theology of liberation. If we priests come to lovingly know Mary, the Queen of prophets and apostles who stands closest to the Servant of Yahweh, then we will have surely taken a giant step toward better understanding and living of our vocation.

# A CLOSING PRAYER

L ord Jesus Christ, for the past fifty-six years you have graciously allowed me to minister to thousands of men who share in the priestly vocation, by teaching, counseling, encouraging, and consoling them. Together, we have learned and, hopefully, will continue to learn how to humbly and courageously follow you, the suffering Servant and Prophet of Yahweh, and how to revere and serve all members of your priestly people worldwide.

Fill us with faith, joy, hope, and deep love! Day by day deepen our capacities to know you more deeply as the nonviolent Servant, the Way of Peace, the Consoler of the afflicted and discouraged! By the power of Spirit, help us to better understand and promote the many avenues of peace, and help each of us to become more clear-sighted and more determined to be, above all, true servants of your Word and humble and joyful ministers to those you have entrusted to us.

Bless our pope and bishops, and all those who enjoy authority in the Church, so that they might better live and creatively foster unity in diversity. Empower all of us to become authentic, holy witnesses to your Truth, and effective instruments in promoting Christian unity and an all-embracing solidarity for the sake of the salvation of the whole world.

# POSTSCRIPT

The text of this book has been written before the Vatican made its declaration that the exclusion of women from the ministerial priesthood is to be considered as an infallible truth. I think that readers by now realize that this is not the case. The worldwide reactions within the whole of Christianity show this clearly.

The main reasons for this worldwide criticism of the use of the category "infallible" are the following:

1. The way of pronouncement of "infallible" does not at all meet the indispensable conditions for an infallible papal doctrine, as laid down at the First Vatican Council (*Pastor aeternus*), namely, that any declaration of infallibility has to be preceded by an inquiry into the convictions of all the faithful, and that thereby "all the means must be used as provided by divine providence." Furthermore, it must be shown that it is based on the Holy Scriptures and the earliest tradition of the Church.

2. Most theologians and especially biblical scholars agree that in Holy Scripture there cannot be found convincing arguments for the positive exclusion of women from the priesthood. The argument that Jesus "did not ordain women" is futile, since nothing at all is said about "ordaining" men. He instituted the Eucharist, entrusting it to the whole of the believers as a supreme gift, mandate, and testament: "Do this, in memory of me—all of you!" It was also most remarkable that Jesus had chosen women to be witnesses and messengers of his Resurrection.

In the text of my book, I avoided speaking for or against the ordination of women, leaving it to the reader to draw conclusions from the basic data of the Bible and from the "signs of the times." I would like, however, to remind the reader that Pope John XXIII not only insisted on vigilance toward the signs of the times but also strongly pointed out that the increased role of women in society, culture, and Church is one of the principal signs of the times.

I think that we should argue kindly and gently about this burning question, with good arguments and a good sense of humor.

BERNARD HÄRING